MW01064689

TABLE OF CONTENTS

Our Story

If you haven't met us before, then we want to introduce ourselves to you.
We want to tell you why and how we went Paleo, how it changed our lives, and why
we're excited about sharing it with you. You can certainly go Paleo without ever
knowing who we are, but we hope that you find our stories helpful and inspiring, and
that you feel comfortable reaching out to us if you ever have questions!

Hi! I'm Louise!

I've always loved eating.

But for most of my life, I hated cooking. In fact, as a girl, one of the requirements I had for my future husband was that he would be a great cook.

Well…Jeremy cooks well. But somehow, I ended up loving cooking more than I ever imagined I would. It's been a complete surprise to me, but it's also been a fun and exciting journey, as I've learned to appreciate both food and health in new and exciting ways.

I grew up in the middle of England, where it's cold, wet, and the food is not known for being either delicious or nutritious. My parents were immigrants from China, and we didn't have very much money, so

they cooked simple meals that didn't cost very much. At the time, I remember wishing that we could eat out more, but looking back, I realize that I was pretty lucky. Although we certainly weren't Paleo (we ate a lot of rice and some bread), most of our meals were reasonably healthy and made from scratch using fresh ingredients.

But as I got older, things started to change. My dad figured out how much he loved sugar, and we used to finish off a tin of biscuits (cookies, if you're American) several times per week. During my last year in high school, my parents moved to America. I stayed in England by myself, and I remember that many of my meals consisted entirely of "cheese on toast" - a toasted piece of bread with a melted piece of processed cheese. And during college at Cambridge, the closest I ever got to cooking was heating up a frozen chicken pot pie.

Eating more and more junk started to take its toll on my body. During law school in New York, I started experiencing more and more health problems. I had constant gastro-intestinal issues, I was always tired, and my skin (which had always been quite clear - even as a teenager) began to break out. At the time, I didn't relate any of this to the food I was eating. It feels funny to look back at now, but I honestly had no idea that most of my health problems were connected at all to the foods I was putting into my body.

While in New York, I went to doctor after doctor in an attempt to start feeling better. I was prescribed dozens of medications, given at least as many opinions, and yet I never seemed to get any better. Not for very long at least.

Fortunately (in some ways), Jeremy has always been a bit obsessed with weight loss. I didn't need to lose any weight but his search eventually led him to a Paleo diet, almost 8 years ago now. I resisted incredibly hard for a while. I couldn't imagine why I'd ever want to give up so many of the foods I loved. From red velvet cake to bread to really good cheese, I was sure that I didn't want to give up any of those things. But Jeremy is nothing if not persistent.

I finally relented and tried a Paleo diet myself. It was REALLY hard at first, and I hated it. I felt like I was always hungry, and I was constantly angry for being deprived of all the foods I wanted. (I blamed Jeremy a lot at that time.)

But after a couple weeks, my body started feeling completely different. I wasn't tired any longer. I didn't feel like I needed a nap every afternoon. My IBS didn't disappear completely, but it got 75% better very quickly. And once I started sleeping enough (in addition to eating well), my skin cleared up. As much as I loved all the foods I was giving up, I loved even more the results I was seeing in my body and my life.

I also began to love cooking. This was, perhaps, a bigger surprise than feeling better. And this wasn't immediate - it probably took me almost a year of being Paleo before I really looked forward to cooking. At first, I tried to re-create all the foods I was used to eating. Some worked out well, and some didn't. But eventually, I just started trying new things. I'd see what fresh meats, fruits, and veggies we had available, and I'd work with whatever I had. It became an experiment and adventure for me.

That adventure continued when I launched AncestralChef.com (now part of **Paleo Flourish Magazine - PaleoMagazine.com**) a couple of years ago. Every week, I'd post a few of the recipes I had created, and week-by-week, more and more people started reading and commenting on my recipes and stories. The more popular it got, the more excited I would get about creating new recipes and helping folks even more.

Today, I can't imagine not being Paleo. I occasionally eat non-Paleo foods, and I don't claim to be anywhere near perfect. But I am much more aware of how these foods affect my life and my body, and I couldn't go back, even if I wanted to. (I don't.)

JEREMY

Hi! I'm Jeremy!

I'm a fat kid at heart. Let me explain.

I was always fat as a kid. I wasn't obese, but we didn't really have obese kids around when I was young, so I was fatter than almost all the other kids. And I hated being the fat kid.

It's hard for me to say whether being fat caused some of my insecurities or whether I just blamed being fat for my insecurities. Regardless, my self-confidence has always been closely tied to how I look. When I feel like I don't look good (when I feel like I'm fat - which is most of the time), I don't feel comfortable with myself or around other people. This has affected my friendships, my relationships with my family, and my romantic relationships.

I remember, in particular, that for most of high school, being sure that the girls I liked would never like me back because I was too chubby. I'd wake up every morning, look in the mirror, and be incredibly angry that I was still fat. I hoped with all my heart that I would wake up one day and not be fat, but I never did

anything about it until I got to college.

When I started college, I decided to change everything. I started running every day, I played sports, and as I thought it was healthy at that time, I went very low-fat. I ate grilled chicken, turkey, lots of bread, and lots of sugar. And because I was young and exercising so much, I started losing weight. In fact, I lost a lot of weight my first year in college. And I was ecstatic about it.

But the next 6-7 years for me were a huge struggle. I'd gain some weight back, lose it again, and then yo-yo back and forth. I'd be able to force myself to eat healthy sometimes, but I was miserable and would frequently go on month-long binges where I'd eat nothing but junk food. I wasn't nourishing my body, I wasn't really taking care of it at all, and I felt tired and unhappy about it the whole time.

One of my strengths (and weaknesses) is that I'm very open to new ideas. So when I first read Loren Cordain's The Paleo Diet, I immediately thought it made sense and jumped on the idea. I'd already been low-carb for a while, and while it was working better than previous diets, I still didn't feel or look the way I wanted to.

I would love to be able to tell you that I started my Paleo diet, loved it, and stuck with it ever since. But that's not the case. For the first 4-5 years, I would stick with it for a couple months, and then I'd abandon ship. I'd go on vacation, or I'd go out partying with friends, or I'd just have a stressful week. Whatever the cause, something would trigger me to abandon the diet and lifestyle that I knew was healthy for me, and for a couple of months, I'd eat junk food.

Unlike many people, there was no moment when everything clicked for me - it was a very long transition. But at some point, I completely stopped wanting foods that make me feel bad (almost all non-Paleo foods).

I still have an innate fear of being fat - I'm not sure if I'll ever completely lose that fear. But by nourishing my body and caring about how I treat it, I'm constantly improving my relationship with my body and myself. Every day, I feel a little more comfortable with how I look and feel, and every day, I'm a little happier about it all.

For me, this is the reason I do everything I do. It's about losing weight and being healthy, but more than anything, it's about helping people care for and love themselves so that they can live a life they love. And hopefully, that journey can start with eating just a little bit better.

WE WANTED A COOKBOOK THAT WE COULD GIVE TO SOMEBODY WHO MAYBE ISN'T FAMILIAR WITH COOKING FROM SCRATCH OR WITH AVOIDING THINGS LIKE GRAINS, LEGUMES, AND PROCESSED SUGARS.

Why We Wrote This Cookbook

We believe that food is medicine and that we can heal our bodies and lives by nourishing our bodies and treating ourselves better.

This cookbook is one step along that journey.

We get hundreds of emails per week from people at various stages of their health journeys. Some are just starting out, some have been trying for years, and some are almost where they want to be.

This cookbook can be used by anybody, but really, it's for folks who are looking to build the foundations of a healthy diet. We wanted a cookbook that we could give to somebody who maybe isn't familiar with cooking from scratch or with avoiding things like grains, legumes, and processed sugars.

To be sure, there are other excellent cookbooks out there - even other excellent Paleo cookbooks. But the main complaint we have about most of them is that we couldn't or wouldn't cook most of the recipes on a daily basis. By and large, the recipes in most cookbooks are too complicated or complex to cook every day.

So we decided to put together a Paleo cookbook of the recipes that we actually prepare and eat on a daily basis. We didn't include 500 recipes because we don't make that many different meals unless it's a special occasion.

Above all else, we decided to make a cookbook that is both practical and amazing. Every recipe in this cookbook is one that we love and make frequently. We've organized them in ways that are easy for you to browse through and find what you're looking for. For most of the recipes, we've included high-resolution images of what it should look like, so that you can know what you're preparing.

And we've included badges, as I'll explain in the next section, in case you're wondering whether certain recipes will work for you in particular.

We hope you love this cookbook!

METRIC MEASUREMENTS

In case you're not living in the United States, we've gone through and converted all measurements to metric, so that you have your choice of how to measure out ingredients.

BADGES

All of our recipes are excellent and 100% Paleo. But we know that you might have conditions that further restrict your diet. While we can't cover everything, we have assigned badges to various recipes to note the following:

Compliant with the Autoimmune Protocol. Recipes with this badge will not contain any eggs, nightshades, or other ingredients that might generally exacerbate an autoimmune condition. Some of these recipes will still have such an ingredient listed, but there will be a note beside the ingredient to omit for AIP. Please note that we have stuck to Sarah Ballantyne's strict AIP ingredients list as published in The Paleo Approach.

Low In Carbohydrates. Recipes with this badge are low in carbohydrates (including Paleo sugars). These are especially great for those with blood sugar issues.

Kid-Friendly. There's no reason why kids (at least those over a year old) couldn't eat every recipe in this book. However, recipes with this badge denote recipes that are particularly appealing to children.

If a recipe has one of these badges, you will see the badge in the lower right-hand corner of the recipe.

GHEE

Ghee is made by evaporating all of the water from butter and then separating the fats from the milk solids. Ghee is the fat.

Because almost all of the milk solids are removed, it has practically no lactose or casein, the 2 components of dairy that cause the most health problems. For this reason, we consider Ghee to be completely Paleo.

However, please be cognizant of how you feel when you use ghee. If you are extremely sensitive to casein, for instance, you may still react to the very small amount of casein in ghee. If you have trouble finding ghee to buy, then you can easily make your own from butter (see recipe on page 178).

MICROWAVES

From our perspective, it doesn't matter at all to us whether or not you choose to use a microwave. Several of our recipes suggest use of a microwave, but there is almost always an alternative listed in such cases.

There are a lot of misconceptions and myths about microwaves, but for our part, we give you the suggestion, because microwaves are often fast and convenient. And if you heat on a low temperature, they often preserve more nutrients than other cooking methods that use higher temperatures.

POTATOES

Very few of the recipes in this book contain potatoes, but we do now consider potatoes to be 100% Paleo. Gram-for-gram, potatoes are quite nutrient-dense, at least equaling sweet potatoes.

The one caveat to all of this is that if you have blood sugar issues, it is probably best to avoid starchy foods like potatoes. But this also extends to sweet potatoes, high-sugar fruits, etc.

EGGS, NUTS, & OTHER FOOD ALLERGIES

There are many Paleo ingredients that are generally healthy, but to which many people are allergic. Examples include eggs, nuts, and shellfish.

We get a lot of questions about how to change various recipes if you're allergic to these ingredients.

In general, we try to offer helpful substitution suggestions whenever possible. However, we couldn't find a good way to substitute a different ingredient in every instance. In many cases, not having one of these ingredients (eggs in particular) makes a recipe nearly impossible to make.

If you have any particular questions about substitutions, please email us, and we will help as much as we can.

SIMPLICITY AND EASE

Above all else, we wrote this cookbook in order to provide you with recipes that we know you will love, but that we also know you'll be able to make every day.

Several of the recipes are almost ridiculously simple, occasionally containing only 2-4 ingredients and often only 2-3 steps.

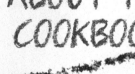

A FEW NOTES ABOUT THIS COOKBOOK

We have worked really hard to make this cookbook as user-friendly as possible. Before you get started, here are some things you should know…

This is not because we couldn't think of more complicated recipes or because we were too lazy to write longer recipes. (It really doesn't take much longer in any case.)

The reason many of our recipes are simple is because we've seen thousands of people try to start Paleo or real-food diets, and the thing that often causes people to fail is that they run out of time or energy to prepare food.

Although complicated recipes often "look" better, we knew that we'd be doing you a disservice by including too many complicated recipes, since even we don't make complicated recipes very long. Usually, we just whip up something quick, often based loosely on one of the recipes in this cookbook.

RE-CREATING NON-PALEO FOODS

If you're just starting a Paleo diet, you'll have a huge urge to try to recreate many of the foods you're used to eating. We understand - we did that for a long time.

And it's not a bad thing to do. Especially if you have a family, it helps ease the transition.

However, we would encourage you, even now, to start thinking about letting go of the breads, pastas, and baked goods. As we now know, once you're able to let them go, you actually stop missing them altogether. There are a few recipes in this cookbook that are re-creations of non-Paleo foods, but by and large, our recipes are designed to be their own dish, not a re-creation.

CONDIMENTS

We debated for a long time whether or not to include condiment recipes in this cookbook. The recipes are quite simple, and you could theoretically do without them.

However, after much thought, we believe that Paleo condiments are an important part of our Paleo cookbook. In fact, in our house, we realized that we make Paleo condiments of one sort or another at least once a week.

ORGANIC, GRASS-FED, AND WILD-CAUGHT

If you can find and afford it, we encourage you to buy meats that are grass-fed (beef and lamb), other meats that are humanely-raised (pork and chicken), fish that are wild-caught, and fruits and vegetables that are organic. In general, all of these adjectives make the food slightly more nutrient-dense, slightly less toxic, and/or a bit more ethical (in terms of how the animal is treated).

However, if you can't afford or find these things, don't shy away from the conventional versions of these foods. The conventional versions are still way better than eating packaged, processed foods.

It's become very popular lately to buy organic foods, and while we agree that it's probably better, it's become popular largely because it's the easy thing to do - not because it's the change that will make the biggest difference for your body.

SUGARS, STARCHES, AND CARBS

Many of our recipes contain fruits or tubers that have a fair amount of sugars or starches (all naturally-occurring, of course). We believe that for most healthy people this is hard to overeat and is pretty good

However, if you know that you are insulin-resistant or have other problems controlling your blood-sugar, then you might want to think about modifying or avoiding these recipes. (Always consult a doctor or medical professional on health issues like insulin-resistance.)

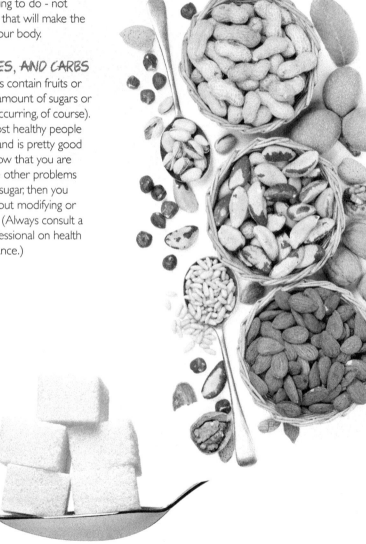

SPECIAL HEALTHY CONDITIONS

As humans, our bodies are all 99.99% the same. And that's important when it comes to nutrition and health.

We all need the same vitamins, minerals, proteins, and fats for our bodies to function like they're supposed to. We all need sleep, exercise, and community.

But once our bodies get broken, what we need often changes a little bit.

For instance, somebody who is highly insulin-resistant, like a Type II Diabetic, still needs all of the things listed above. But that person also needs to control their blood sugar in ways that would happen automatically in a healthy body.

Likewise, someone who has an autoimmune disease like Lupus, Hashimoto's, or Crohn's will likely need to avoid foods like eggs and tomatoes initially in order to allow their body to heal.

Those are just 2 examples, and there are countless others. We designed the recipes in this cookbook to be as healthy as possible, but there's no way we could ensure that the recipes will be the best ones for every health condition.

If you have diabetes, an autoimmune disease, or any other condition, please do 2 things. First of all, consult your doctor or other medical professional (consider finding a naturopath or Paleo practioner). We believe in food as medicine, but we also still believe in modern medicine. Secondly, start paying close attention to how you feel when you eat certain foods. If you want to be serious about it, keep a journal or diary of how you feel after various meals. That knowledge is invaluable when it comes to healing your body.

BUT ONCE OUR BODIES
GET BROKEN, WHAT WE
NEED OFTEN CHANGES
A LITTLE BIT.

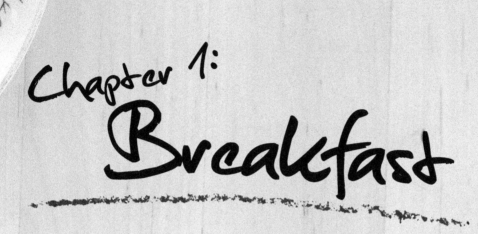

Chapter 1:
Breakfast

2-Ingredient Pancakes

Prep Time: 2 minutes
Cook Time: 20 minutes
Total Time: 22 minutes
Yield: 1 serving
Serving Size: 1 pancake

These pancakes are so simple and yet so amazing. The bananas make them absolutely addictive. It takes a little while to cook the pancakes, so we suggest using 2 pans at once if you can.

INGREDIENTS

- 1 banana, peeled
- 1 egg
- 1 Tablespoon (15 ml) coconut oil

INSTRUCTIONS

1. Blend the egg and the banana in a blender to form a batter.
2. Place 1 tablespoon of coconut oil into a frying pan and pour in the batter to create a thin pancake (smaller pancakes are easier to flip).
3. Let the pancake cook for around 10 minutes before flipping it carefully.
4. After flipping it, let the other side cook for around 10 minutes.

Almond Butter Chocolate Shake

Prep Time: 5 minutes
Cook Time: 0 minutes
Total Time: 5 minutes
Yield: 1 serving
Serving Size: 1 cup

This might sound a little surprising, but the absolute hardest thing for Jeremy to give up was milkshakes. There's no food that he loves more. So we had to try a few times to re-create something similar. This was one of our favorites, and we don't think you'll be disappointed.

INGREDIENTS

- 1 cup *(8 oz, 240 ml)* coconut milk or almond milk
- 2 Tablespoons *(15 g)* no-sugar added cacao powder
- 1 Tablespoon *(16 g)* almond butter
- 1 teaspoon *(7 g)* raw honey (omit for D or use stevia)
- 1 teaspoon *(5 ml)* vanilla extract
- ¼ cup *(2 oz, 35 g)* ice (optional)

INSTRUCTIONS

1. Place all the ingredients into a blender and blend well.

SUBSTITUTIONS

• Chocolate whey protein powder can be used instead of cacao powder for extra protein. Check ingredients in the whey protein powder.

Sweet Potato Breakfast Hash

Prep Time: 10 minutes
Cook Time: 5 minutes
Total Time: 15 minutes
Yield: 2 servings
Serving Size: 1 plate

This breakfast recipe is a fantastic way to use any leftover meats from the night before. It's also a great opportunity to add in your favorite herbs.

INGREDIENTS

- 1 sweet potato, shredded
- ½ zucchini, shredded
- 1 cup leftover meat, shredded *(approx. 6 oz)*
- 1 Tablespoon *(2 g)* fresh thyme leaves, finely chopped *(or use 1 tsp (1 g) dried thyme or use other herbs of your choosing)*
- 1 Tablespoons *(15 ml)* coconut oil for cooking
- Salt to taste

INSTRUCTIONS

1. Place 1 Tablespoon of coconut oil into a frying pan on medium heat.
2. Add in the shredded sweet potato, shredded zucchini, and left over meat. Cook until the sweet potato starts to get tender (approx. 5 minutes).
3. Add in the herbs and salt to taste.

SUBSTITUTIONS

- Bacon or other deli meat can be used if you don't have any leftover meats.

Chocolate Avocado Smoothie

Prep Time: 5-10 minutes
Cook Time: 0 minutes
Total Time: 5-10 minutes
Yield: 2 servings
Serving Size: 1 large glass

For the most part, we always try to eat whole foods, cooked from scratch. But we also love smoothies like this because the ingredients are still unprocessed and nutritious, but the total time to make and drink a smoothie is so short, and like most people, we often feel like we're running out of time.

INGREDIENTS

- 1 avocado
- 2 frozen bananas
- ½ cup *(70 g)* frozen raspberries *(or fresh raspberries or other berries)*
- 1-2 Tablespoons *(5-10 g)* unsweetened cacao powder *(use carob powder for AIP)*
- 2 cups *(480 ml)* almond milk or coconut milk *(use coconut milk for AIP)*

INSTRUCTIONS

1. If you have unpeeled frozen bananas, then take the frozen bananas from the freezer and leave to thaw for 10 minutes before peeling *(or cut the skin off with a paring knife)*.
2. Place all the ingredients into a blender and blend well.

Chocolate Coconut Pancakes

Prep Time: 10 minutes
Cook Time: 30 minutes
Total Time: 40 minutes
Yield: 4-5 servings
Serving Size: 2-3 pancakes

There are 2 pancake recipes in this cookbook. One might have been enough, but we couldn't leave this one out because it's just too good. Especially if you love chocolate!

INGREDIENTS

- 4 eggs
- ½ cup *(60g)* coconut flour
- 1 cup *(240 ml)* coconut milk
- 2 teaspoons *(10 ml)* vanilla extract
- 2-3 Tablespoons *(42-63 g)* raw honey *(omit or use stevia for D)*
- 1 teaspoon *(5 g)* baking soda
- ¼ cup *(22 g)* unsweetened cacao powder
- Coconut oil *(or ghee)* for cooking
- Raw honey *(or maple syrup)* for drizzling *(optional - omit for D)*

INSTRUCTIONS

1. Beat the eggs. While beating, add in the coconut flour, coconut milk, vanilla extract, raw honey, baking soda, and cacao powder. Mix well.
2. Put some coconut oil onto a griddle or frying pan on low heat.
3. Ladle some of the batter into the pan *(to form a 3-inch diameter circle)*. The pancake should be a bit thick so no need to try to make the batter spread out much. If you're using a large enough frying pan, you can cook 3 or 4 pancakes at the same time.
4. Cook for 10 minutes on each side - flip with a large spatula. Keep on low heat so it doesn't burn.
5. The pancakes can be a bit dry by themselves, so have it with some raw honey/maple syrup/ghee/coconut oil/fruit.

Creamy Breakfast Porridge

Prep Time: 5 minutes
Cook Time: 10 minutes
Total Time: 15 minutes
Yield: 1 serving
Serving Size: 1 bowl

Breakfast is the meal that we get asked about most often. It was a big deal for us for a long time *(now we mostly eat leftovers for breakfast)*, but this is one of the recipes that's easy and filling in the morning. It's also fast in case you don't have much time.

INGREDIENTS

- ½ cup *(50 g)* almonds, ground using a food processor or blender
- ¾ cup *(177 ml)* coconut cream *(or, alternatively use the top layer of cream from a refrigerated can of coconut milk)*
- 1 teaspoon *(7 g)* raw honey *(omit or use stevia for D)*
- 1 teaspoon *(3 g)* cinnamon powder
- Dash of nutmeg
- Dash of cloves
- Dash of cardamom *(optional)*

INSTRUCTIONS

1. Heat the coconut cream in a small saucepan on medium heat until it forms a liquid.
2. Add in the ground almonds and honey, and stir to mix.
3. Keep stirring for approximately 5 minutes *(it'll start to thicken a bit more)*.
4. Add in the spices *(have a taste to check whether you want more sweetener or spices)* and serve hot.

Easy Bacon Cups

Prep Time: 15 minutes
Cook Time: 25 minutes
Total Time: 40 minutes
Yield: 3 servings
Serving Size: 2 bacon cups

You can add pretty much anything into these cups - guacamole, diced avocados, salsa, or even scrambled eggs.

INGREDIENTS

- 15 thin slices of bacon
- Equipment: standard nonstick metal muffin or cupcake pan

INSTRUCTIONS

1. Preheat oven to 400 F *(204 C)*.
2. Each bacon cup will require 2 and ½ slices of bacon, to be used as described in Step #3 below.
3. Start by turning the entire muffin/cupcake pan over, so that the side that is normally the bottom is on top. To make 1 bacon cup, place 2 half slices of bacon across the back of one of the muffin/cupcake cups, both in the same direction. Then, place another half slice across those 2, perpendicular to the direction of the first 2 half slices. Finally, wrap a whole slice of bacon tightly around the sides of the cup. The slice wrapped around the sides will help to hold the bottom pieces of bacon together.
4. Repeat Step #3 for the other 5 cups. *(You can scale this recipe to as many cups as your pan has by simply using more bacon.)*
5. Place the entire pan *(still upside-down)* into the oven and bake for 25 minutes until crispy *(place a baking tray underneath in the oven to catch any dripping bacon fat).*
6. Cool for 5-10 minutes, and then carefully remove the bacon cups from the muffin tray.

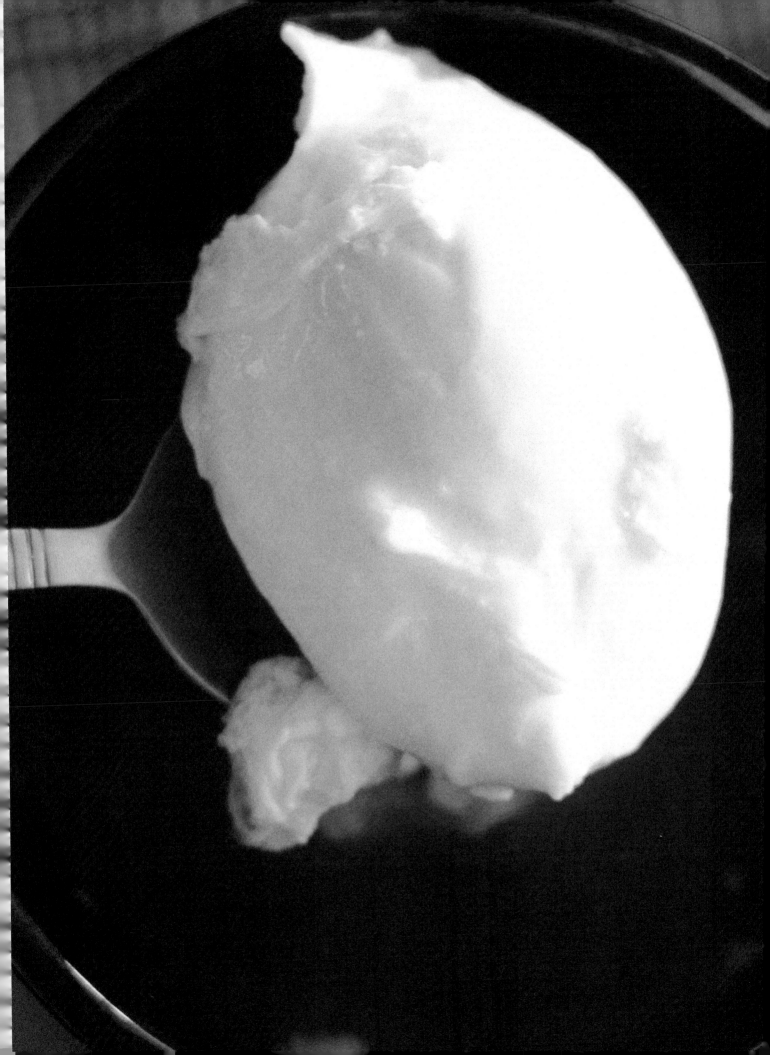

Fool-proof Poached Egg

Prep Time: 5 minutes
Cook Time: 5 minutes
Total Time: 10 minutes
Yield: 1 serving
Serving Size: 1 poached egg

Some dishes are just fun and cool to make *(partially because most people can't do it very well)*. You can go read a lot about how to properly make a poached egg, but this is the only way we've ever found to do it consistently.

INGREDIENTS

- 1 egg
- 2-3 teaspoons *(10-15 ml)* apple cider vinegar or lemon juice *(optional)*

INSTRUCTIONS

1. Crack an egg into a bowl.
2. Heat a saucepan with at least 3 inches of water.
3. Add the vinegar or lemon juice into the water
4. After the water boils, turn down the heat a bit so that it stops boiling.
5. Use a spoon to start stirring the water in the saucepan to create a whirlpool *(i.e., stir in a circle)*.
6. Drop the egg into the water while the water is still spinning.
7. Leave to cook on a medium heat so that the water isn't boiling. For a soft but not-runny poached egg, cook in the water for 5 minutes. If you prefer a runny poached egg, then remove from the water after around 3 minutes.

Fruit n' Nut Granola

Prep Time: 10 minutes
Cook Time: 0 minutes
Total Time: 10 minutes
Yield: 1 serving
Serving Size: 1 small bowl

Another fast and simple recipe. If you search for just 5 minutes on Google, you can find a lot of different Paleo granola recipes, and many of them are good. But a lot of them require too much work for something that we usually want quickly. This one isn't instant, but it doesn't take long to get a delicious result. Plus you can make large batches of this to make your Paleo breakfast effortless.

INGREDIENTS

- ½ cup *(50 g)* almonds *(or other nut of your choice)*
- ½ cup *(50 g)* pumpkin seeds *(or other seed of your choice)*
- 15 raisins *(omit or use stevia for D)*
- 1 prune, chopped *(optional - omit for D)*
- *(Serve with coconut milk or almond milk)*

INSTRUCTIONS

1. Place the almonds and pumpkin seeds into a blender or food processor and blend on a slow setting so that they're in reasonably large chunks still.
2. Pour the blended nuts/seeds into a bowl and top with the dried fruit.
3. Pour cold coconut milk or regular milk on top and enjoy.

SUBSTITUTIONS

- You may substitute any nut/seed for the almonds and pumpkin seeds or add in additional ones.

Perfect Green Smoothie

Prep Time: 5 minutes
Cook Time: 0 minutes
Total Time: 5 minutes
Yield: 1 serving
Serving Size: 1 cup

Of all the recipes in this cookbook, we make this one most often. It's an easy breakfast, but more importantly, it's a great way to get both more greens and more resistant starch (read this article for more on resistant starch) into your diet, both of which are excellent for your overall health. Plus, this smoothie is much tastier than you'd ever imagine.

INGREDIENTS

- 1 cup *(240 ml)* coconut milk
  (if you can't find fresh, refrigerated coconut milk, then use almond milk or even water)
- 2 large handfuls of spinach or kale
  (the amount does not need to be exact - you can also blanche them first to reduce the anti-nutrients)
- 1 Tablespoon *(15 ml)* coconut oil
- 1 ripe banana
- 1/3 cup *(~45 g)* almonds *(pre-soaked is even better) (omit for AIP)*
- 7-8 *(~20 g)* brazil nuts *(omit for AIP)*
- 1 Tablespoon *(8 g)* potato starch *(omit for AIP)*
- 1 Tablespoon *(8 g)* pure whey protein *(omit if very sensitive to dairy or AIP)*

INSTRUCTIONS

1. Place all ingredients except for potato starch and whey protein into a blender and blend well.
2. After the initial mixture is blended well, add in the whey protein and potato starch and blend well.

Perfectly Scrambled Eggs

Prep Time: 0 minutes
Cook Time: 10 minutes
Total Time: 10 minutes
Yield: 1 serving
Serving Size: 3-egg scramble

This is a recipe inspired by Gordon Ramsay. You probably think you know how to scramble eggs *(and what scrambled eggs are supposed to taste like)*. But you probably don't. Follow the instructions below exactly, and see the difference for yourself.

INGREDIENTS

- 3 eggs *(do not whisk! – this is very important!)*
- 2 Tablespoons (30 ml) coconut oil *(or ghee)*
- Salt and pepper, to taste

INSTRUCTIONS

1. Prior to placing the saucepan on the stove, crack the eggs into the saucepan and add the coconut oil to the saucepan as well.
2. Place the saucepan on medium heat and start stirring so that the eggs get broken up.
3. Keep stirring without stopping.
4. Move the saucepan off the heat when you start to see some of the egg sticking to the bottom of the saucepan. While off of the heat, keep stirring for about 10 seconds and then put the saucepan back onto the heat for another 20-30 seconds, but always keep stirring. The goal is to not overcook the eggs!
5. Repeat Step #4 three or four times until you see that the mixture becomes more solid *(but don't wait until it's actually solid!)*.
6. Once the eggs have solidified a bit, take the pot off the heat permanently.
7. Lastly, season with salt and pepper and serve immediately.

Sweet n' Salty Bacon Egg Muffins

Prep Time: 10 minutes
Cook Time: 30 minutes
Total Time: 40 minutes
Yield: 6 servings
Serving Size: 2 muffins

Sometimes, we know we're going to be out (for instance, traveling or at a conference), and we know that there won't be much we're willing to eat. In those cases, we often make these egg muffins to take with us. You shouldn't keep them out of the refrigerator for too long, but we routinely eat them 6-8 hours after we make them.

INGREDIENTS

- 4 eggs
- ½ cup *(120 ml)* coconut cream *(or, alternatively use the top layer of cream from a refrigerated can of coconut milk)*
- 1 cup *(128 g)* carrots
  (approx. 1 large carrot), shredded (I used my food processor's shredding attachment)
- ½ cup *(16 g)* cooked bacon, broken into bits
- Bacon fat for greasing muffin pan, or use silicone muffin pan or muffin cup liners

INSTRUCTIONS

1. Preheat oven to 350 F *(177 C)*.
2. Mix all the ingredients together well in a large mixing bowl *(I use an electric mixer)*.
3. Pour into muffin cups so that there's an equal amount in each cup.
4. Bake for 30 minutes.
5. Let cool. Enjoy immediately or store in refrigerator for up to 5-7 days.

Blueberry Mint Smoothie

Prep Time: 5 minutes
Cook Time: 0 minutes
Total Time: 5 minutes
Yield: 1 serving
Serving Size: 1 glass

Smoothies make such an easy and delicious breakfast, and this smoothie is a great one to start your day with - it's got plenty of healthy fats and only a small amount of sugar from the blueberries.

INGREDIENTS

- ½ cup *(70 g)* frozen blueberries
- ½ cup *(240 ml)* coconut milk (or water)
- 1 teaspoon mint tea leaves (or use approx. 10 fresh mint leaves)
- ½ avocado
- ¾ cup of ice

INSTRUCTIONS

1. Add everything to the blender.
2. Blend well.

Steamed Egg Custard

Prep Time: 5 minutes
Cook Time: 15 minutes
Total Time: 20 minutes
Yield: 1 serving
Serving Size: 1 bowl

Louise's mom used to make this recipe for her when she was growing up, and Louise has always loved it. But if you don't have a steamer, don't worry - we've got instructions for how to create your own steamer below.

INGREDIENTS

- 2 eggs
- Room-temperature water
- 1 Tablespoon *(15 ml)* tamari soy sauce
- 1 teaspoon *(5 ml)* sesame oil
- 1 Tablespoon *(4 g)* scallions (chopped green onions)

INSTRUCTIONS

1. Place the 2 eggs into a small bowl. Add room-temperature water (approx. same volume as the eggs).
2. Mix well.
3. Remove the foam that forms at the top of the bowl.
4. Place into a steamer (the water in the steamer should be boiling already) for 10-12 minutes.
5. Check to make sure the middle of the custard isn't a liquid anymore. Cook for a few minutes longer if necessary.
6. Serve with tamari soy sauce, sesame oil, and scallions as toppings.

SUBSTITUTIONS

• If you don't have a steamer, don't worry, you can make your own steamer by using a tall saucepan and an old bowl. Fill the saucepan 1/3 of the way with water, place the old bowl upside down in the saucepan so that it's almost submerged in the water, and then place the bowl or plate you want to steam on top of the old bowl. Make sure the lid to the saucepan still fits and you're ready to go.

Chapter 2:
Appetizers

Autumn Butternut Squash Soup

Prep Time: 15 minutes
Cook Time: 1 hour 30 minutes
Total Time: 1 hour 45 minutes
Yield: 4 servings
Serving Size: 1 bowl

Louise came up with this recipe on an autumn day when we'd bought a lot of butternut squash, and we needed to eat it before it went bad. We'd love to tell you that all of our recipes are well planned out in advance, but it's not always the case. This one turned out marvelously, and we've made it many times since.

INGREDIENTS

- 1 medium sized onion *(or half a large one)*, chopped
- 32 fluid ounces *(950 ml)* chicken broth *(or bone broth – see page 168 for recipe)*
- 1 whole butternut squash
- 1 Tablespoon *(15 ml)* coconut oil
- Salt to taste
- Nutmeg and pepper *(optional - omit both for AIP)*

INSTRUCTIONS

1. Add 1 Tablespoon of coconut oil to a large pot and sauté the chopped onions until they turn translucent.
2. While the onions are cooking, chop up the butternut squash *(e.g, into 1-inch thick pieces)*, remove the seeds, and then remove the skin with a sharp knife.
3. Add the chopped butternut squash and chicken broth to the pot and simmer on a medium heat for 1 hour.
4. Use an immersion blender to puree the cooked veggies. *(Try to keep the end of the stick immersed in the soup to prevent too much splashing)* If you don't have an immersion blender, then you can take the softened veggies out of the pot and place them into a blender or food processor to puree.
5. Once pureed, season the soup with salt, nutmeg, and pepper.

SUBSTITUTIONS

- The butternut squash can be substituted with sweet potatoes or pumpkin.

the *Essential* **PALEO** COOKBOOK

47

Bacon Wrapped Dates Stuffed with Cashew 'Cheese'

Prep Time: 15 minutes *(however, cashews should be soaked overnight before using)*
Cook Time: 30 minutes
Total Time: 45 minutes
Yield: 4 servings
Serving Size: 4 dates

We used to make these bacon-wrapped dates with blue cheese, but we don't eat cheese any longer. You wouldn't imagine it, but the cashews actually turn out quite well as a substitute for cheese. The only problem with this recipe is that 16 dates probably won't last very long for you.

INGREDIENTS

- 16 pitted dates *(small) (scale up the cashew and coconut oil amounts for larger dates)*
- 8 slices of thinly sliced bacon *(cut each slice in half to create 16 shorter slices)*
- ½ cup *(60 g)* raw cashews, soaked overnight *(omit for AIP)*
- 1 Tablespoon *(15 ml)* coconut oil
- ½ cup *(118 ml)* water

INSTRUCTIONS

1. Place the raw cashews into a bowl of room temperature water so that it covers the cashews, drape a paper towel or tea towel over the bowl to prevent dust settling, and soak overnight.
2. Preheat oven to 350 F *(177 C)*.
3. Place the soaked cashews, 1/2 cup fresh water, and coconut oil into a blender and blend until smooth.
4. Slice each date along one side so that it opens up and fill each date with the cashew 'cheese' and close it up. Wrap one of the half-slices of bacon around the date and place on baking tray with sides *(as the fat from the bacon tends to run)*.
5. Bake for 20 minutes before flipping the bacon-wrapped dates over *(with tongs)*.
6. Bake for another 10 minutes *(i.e. for a total of 30 minutes)*.

Balsamic Fruit Salad

Prep Time: 10 minutes
Cook Time: 0 minutes
Total Time: 10 minutes
Yield: 2 servings
Serving Size: 1 cup

Louise loves salads in the summer, and Jeremy is starting to like them a little more… But pretty much everybody loves this fruit salad, because it's really refreshing and delicious.

INGREDIENTS

- ½ lb *(227 g)* cherry or grape tomatoes *(omit for AIP)*
- 1 peach *(ripe, but not too soft)*
- Handful of blueberries
- 4 fresh basil leaves, thinly sliced
- ½ Tablespoon *(7 ml)* of balsamic vinegar
- 2 Tablespoons *(30 ml)* of olive oil

INSTRUCTIONS

1. Peel the peach *(I used a potato peeler)* and then dice it.
2. Halve each cherry or grape tomato.
3. Toss all ingredients together in a bowl and serve.

SUBSTITUTIONS

- Cucumbers can be substituted for the tomatoes.
- Other berries can be substituted for the blueberries.

Carrot Crab Hash with Ginger and Cilantro

Prep Time: 10 minutes
Cook Time: 20 minutes
Total Time: 30 minutes
Yield: 4-6 servings
Serving Size: Approx. 1 cup

Obviously we like all of the recipes in this cookbook. But we worry that certain of our favorite recipes will get overlooked because they're not "typical" recipes. Please do not overlook this carrot and crab hash. It's amazing, and all of our friends who try it agree.

INGREDIENTS

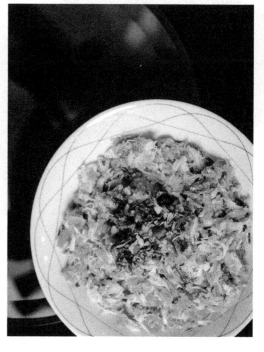

- 2 carrots, peeled and shredded
- 1 lb *(454 g)* lump crabmeat *(fresh or canned)*
- ¼ cup *(25 g)* scallions *(green onions)* chopped
- 2 boiled eggs, diced *(optional - omit for AIP)*
- ¼ cup *(4 g)* cilantro, finely chopped
- 2 cloves garlic, crushed
- 2 teaspoons *(4 g)* fresh ginger, grated
- 1 Tablespoon *(15 ml)* lemon juice
- Salt to taste
- 2-4 Tablespoons *(30-60 ml)* coconut oil

INSTRUCTIONS

1. Place 2-4 Tablespoons of coconut oil into a frying pan *(or a saucepan)*, and sauté the carrots on medium-high heat until they start to soften (add more coconut oil as the carrots soak it up). This takes approx. 15 minutes.
2. Add in the crabmeat, scallions, and boiled eggs and sauté for 5-10 minutes more.
3. Lastly, add the cilantro, garlic, ginger, lemon juice, and salt to taste. Sauté for a few minutes more to combine the flavors.
4. Serve immediately.

SUBSTITUTIONS

- Chicken breast *(finely diced)* can be used instead of crabmeat, but you should cook it separately before adding to the carrots.
- Scrambled eggs can be used instead of boiled eggs.
- Apple cider vinegar can be used instead of lemon juice.

50

Chinese Bamboo Salad

Prep Time: 5 minutes
Cook Time: 0 minutes
Total Time: 5 minutes
Yield: 2 servings
Serving Size: 1/2 cup

This is a really easy Chinese dish to recreate at home. You can usually find canned bamboo shoots in Asian supermarkets as well as some larger regular supermarkets. This dish works best with sesame oil, but if you can't find any sesame oil, then olive oil works too.

INGREDIENTS
- 1 8-ounce *(227 g)* can of sliced bamboo shoots
- 2 Tablespoons *(2 g)* cilantro, finely chopped
- 1 Tablespoon *(15 ml)* sesame oil *(use olive oil for AIP)*
- Salt to taste

INSTRUCTIONS
1. Drain the bamboo shoots and toss with the cilantro, sesame oil, and salt.

SUBSTITUTIONS
• Sliced, lightly boiled/steamed asparagus can be used instead of bamboo shoots.

Coconut Plantain Chips

Prep Time: 15 minutes
Cook Time: 30 minutes
Total Time: 45 minutes
Yield: 2 servings
Serving Size: 1 small bowl

In the US, it seems like chips *(potato chips, corn chips, etc.)* are a whole category of foods. So when we went Paleo, we didn't know what to snack on. We'll warn you that these plantain chips are a little addictive and take a bit of effort to make, but if you want a good snack, this is where to start. They're also a great way to start a meal.

INGREDIENTS

- 2 plantains (green or ripe), peeled and sliced as thin as possible
- Approx. ½ cup (118 ml) coconut oil *(depends how big the saucepan is)*
- Salt to taste
- Cumin powder *(or paprika)* to taste *(omit for AIP)*

INSTRUCTIONS

1. Place the coconut oil into a saucepan so that it's approx. 1/4 inch deep *(or use a deep fat fryer)*.
2. Heat up the oil for 3-4 minutes on a medium heat.
3. Drop in each thin slice of plantain one by one into the oil so they're not overlapping.
4. Use a perforated spoon to get the slices out as soon as they turn golden.
5. Repeat until all the slices are fried
6. Dust with salt and cumin *(or paprika)* to taste and mix well without breaking any of the chips!

SUBSTITUTIONS:

- Use sweet potatoes instead of plantains to make sweet potato chips.
- Bananas can be used instead of plantains.

52

Fiery Buffalo Wings

Prep Time: 15 minutes
Cook Time: 45 minutes
Total Time: 1 hour
Yield: 4 servings
Serving Size: 3 wings

Like everyone else, we still love hanging out with friends for parties or big sporting events. And we need things to snack on. Buffalo wings are almost Paleo to begin with, although they're often coated with butter and flour. So we decided to create our own. Here they are - adjust the hot sauce amount for your level of spice.

INGREDIENTS

- 12 small chicken wings
- ½ cup *(60 g)* coconut flour
- ½ teaspoon *(1 g)* cayenne pepper
- ½ teaspoon *(1 g)* black pepper
- ½ teaspoon *(1 g)* crushed red pepper flakes
- 1 Tablespoon *(7 g)* paprika
- 1 Tablespoon *(8 g)* garlic powder
- 1 Tablespoon *(18 g)* salt
- ¼ cup *(60 ml)* ghee, melted
- ¼ cup *(56 ml)* hot sauce

INSTRUCTIONS

1. Preheat oven to 400 F *(204 C)*.
2. Mix the coconut flour, dried spices, and salt together in a bowl.
3. Coat each chicken wing with the coconut flour mixture. Refrigerate for 15-30 minutes to help the flour stick a bit better to the wings *(optional)*.
4. Grease a baking tray *(or line it with aluminum foil)*.
5. Mix the ghee and the hot sauce together well.
6. Dip each chicken wing into the ghee and hot sauce mixture and place onto the baking tray.
7. Bake for 45 minutes.

SUBSTITUTIONS

- Butter (if you tolerate dairy) or coconut oil can be used instead of ghee.
- If you omit any spices, increase the amount of garlic powder.

Hearty Cauliflower, Leek & Bacon Soup

Prep Time: 10 minutes
Cook Time: 1 hour
Total Time: 1 hour 10 minutes
Yield: 4 servings
Serving Size: 1 cup

Cauliflower is really cool. You can use it to make "rice" dishes *(we have a couple recipes in this cookbook)*, or you can use it to replicate potatoes. In soups, this comes in very handy. This soup is a great fall/winter soup. The leek and bacon add most of the flavor, and the cauliflower provides the thicker texture.

INGREDIENTS

- ½ head of cauliflower
- 6 cups *(1.4 l)* of chicken broth *(or vegetable broth)*
- 1 leek
- 5 strips of bacon, cooked
- Salt and pepper *(omit for AIP)* to taste

INSTRUCTIONS

1. Cut the cauliflower and leek into small pieces.
2. Place the cauliflower and leek into a pot with the chicken broth.
3. Cover the pot and simmer for 1 hour or until tender.
4. Use an immersion blender to puree the vegetables to create a smooth soup. *(If you don't have an immersion blender, you can take the vegetables out, let cool briefly, puree in a normal blender, and then put back into the pot.)*
5. Break the cooked bacon into small pieces and drop into the soup.
6. Add salt and pepper to taste.

SUBSTITUTIONS

- Onion can be used instead of leek *(use 1 small white or yellow onion)*.

Splendid Strawberry Spinach Salad

Prep Time: 10 minutes
Cook Time: 0 minutes
Total Time: 10 minutes
Yield: 4 servings
Serving Size: 1 small bowl

You don't really need very many salad recipes. In general, you can just throw in whatever you like into a salad. But we wanted to include this one, because it's a very simple base that you can use over and over again by adding different things *(walnuts, cucumbers, etc.)*.

INGREDIENTS

- 2 ounces *(57 g or approx. 4-6 handfuls)* baby spinach leaves, washed
- 10 medium-sized strawberries
- Strawberry salad dressing *(see page 176 for recipe)*

INSTRUCTIONS

1. Slice up the 10 strawberries and add to a large bowl with the spinach. Toss with dressing.

SUBSTITUTIONS

- Other berries can be used instead of strawberries

Sweet and Spicy Tuna Salad

Prep Time: 15 minutes
Cook Time: 0 minutes
Total Time: 15 minutes
Yield: 4 servings
Serving Size: ½ cup

We use curry powder and garam masala a ton *(check out our green bean and apple recipe as well)* - we love the flavor these spices add. Tuna salad is good in its own right, but when you spice it up and add a little sweetness, it's magical.

INGREDIENTS

- 1 lb *(454 g)* canned tuna
- 1 apple, peeled and diced
- ½ cup *(30 g)* parsley, finely chopped
- ½ cup (120 g) coconut mayo *(see page 172 for recipe)*
- 2 Tablespoons *(13 g)* curry powder
- 1 Tablespoon *(18 g)* salt *(or to taste)*

INSTRUCTIONS

1. Add the tuna, diced apple, parsley, coconut mayo, curry powder, and salt to the mixing bowl.
2. Mix well.

Thai Lemongrass Shrimp Soup

Prep Time: 10 minutes
Cook Time: 30 minutes
Total Time: 40 minutes
Yield: 4 servings
Serving Size: 1 bowl

This might not be the kind of dish you normally cook, but we encourage you to branch out a little. It's relatively quick to make, and soups like this are always excellent, particularly if you're having people over that you want to impress.

INGREDIENTS

- 16 Large Shrimp *(approx. 1 lb (454 g))*
- 2-3 cups *(473-710 ml)* of coconut cream *(or, alternatively use the top layer of cream from a refrigerated can of coconut milk)*
- 1 quart *(947 ml)* chicken broth
- 3 large button mushrooms, sliced
- 1 lemongrass stalk, split down the center and then chopped into 2-inch long chunks
- 1 teaspoon *(2 g)* ginger, freshly grated *(traditional recipe uses thin slices of galangal)*
- 1 small Thai chili (optional), finely diced *(omit for AIP)*
- 3 Tablespoons *(45 ml)* fish sauce
- Juice of ½ of a lime
- Salt to taste
- 2 Tablespoons *(2 g)* cilantro, finely chopped *(for garnish)*

INSTRUCTIONS

1. Heat the chicken stock in a medium-sized pot and add in the mushrooms, lemongrass, ginger, chili, fish sauce, and lime juice.
2. Simmer for 10 minutes.
3. Add in the coconut cream and simmer for another 10 minutes until the coconut cream mixes in well.
4. Taste the broth and add in salt to taste. Add in more fish sauce, lime juice, or coconut cream depending on how you like the soup.
5. Add in the shrimp and simmer for 8-10 minutes.
6. Serve immediately with the cilantro as garnish.

SUBSTITUTIONS

- Chicken breast cut into small chunks can be used instead of shrimp.
- Almond milk can be used instead of coconut milk *(but the soup will not be as creamy)*.
- Water, bone broth, or any other stock can be used instead of chicken stock.
- Instead of button mushrooms, you can use straw or shiitake mushrooms.

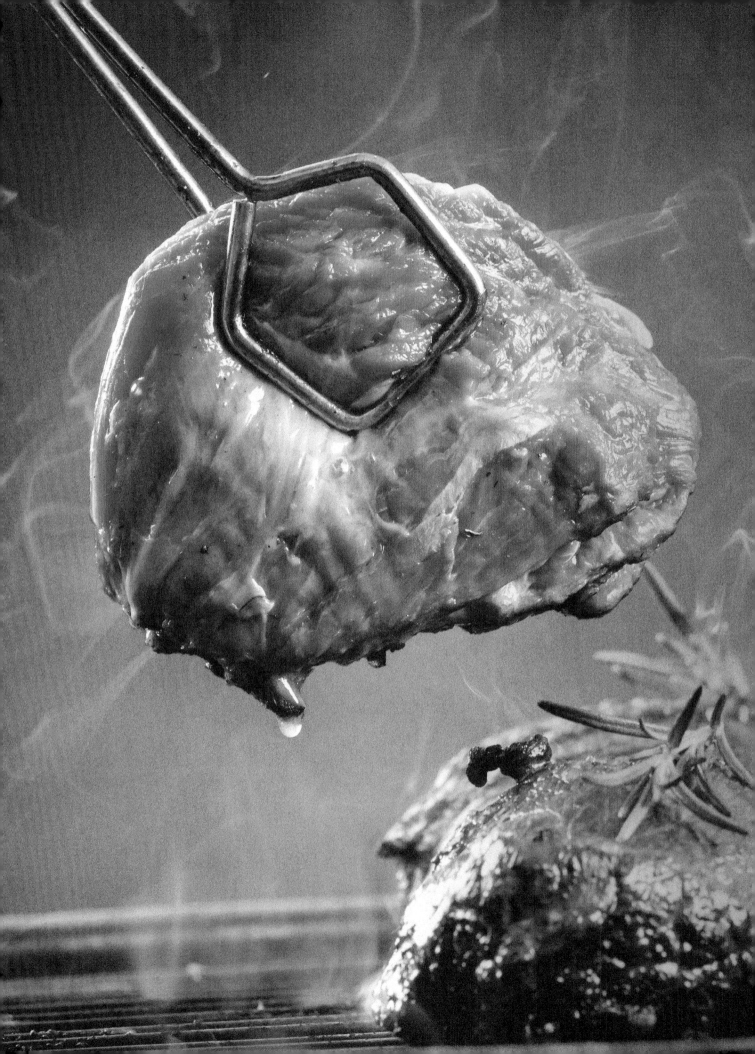

Chapter 3: Entrees

Bacon Acorn Squash Mash

Prep Time: 10 minutes
Cook Time: 50 minutes
Total Time: 1 hour
Yield: 2 servings
Serving Size: 1 large bowl

This recipe is named for the Acorn Squash, but it's really the bacon and collard greens that make all the difference. If you recall, Jeremy grew up in Georgia, and collard greens with either bacon or ham hock are a staple there.

INGREDIENTS

- 1 lb *(454 g)* bacon, uncooked, chopped into small pieces
- 10 ounces *(284 g)* collard greens *(approx. 1 bunch)*, chopped into small pieces
- 2 medium-sized acorn squash
- ½ navel orange, peeled and finely chopped
- Pinch of saffron *(optional - crush and soak for 30 minutes in warm water)*

INSTRUCTIONS

1. Halve the acorn squash and remove the seeds. Soften the inside of the squash by baking on a baking tray in the oven for 40 minutes at 400 F *(204 C)* or microwave on high for 3-4 minutes.
2. Cook the bacon pieces in a pot until crispy.
3. Boil the collard greens in a pot of boiling water for 40 minutes until tender. Add to the pot with the bacon.
4. Scoop out the inside of the acorn squash when it's tender and place into the pot with the bacon pieces and the collard greens.
5. Add the orange and saffron *(optional)* to the pot and cook on a low heat. Stir until the acorn squash forms a mash consistency *(5-10 minutes)*. Serve immediately.

SUBSTITUTIONS

- Butternut squash can be used instead of acorn squash.

Pressure Cooker Chicken Stew

Prep Time: 15 minutes
Cook Time: 35 minutes
Total Time: 50 minutes
Yield: 2-3 servings
Serving Size: 1 bowl

Sometimes it can be really comforting to have a bowl of chicken stew. This is especially true for Louise during the winter months. If you don't have a pressure cooker, don't worry, you can use a slow cooker for this recipe - just set it for 8 hours on low heat.

INGREDIENTS

- 2-3 chicken breasts *(approx. 1 lb or 450 g)*, diced
- 4 cups *(1 l)* chicken broth or water
- 2 small carrots, chopped
- 3 stalks of celery, chopped
- 1 teaspoon *(5 ml)* tamari sauce *(use coconut aminos for AIP)*
- ½ Tablespoon *(1 g)* fresh thyme leaves *(or use ½ tsp (0.5 g) dried thyme)*
- ½ cup parsley, chopped and divided (save half for when you're serving the stew)
- 1 Tablespoon *(7 g)* unflavored gelatin powder (optional)
- Salt to taste
- Arrowroot flour/powder for thickening *(optional - omit for D)*

INSTRUCTIONS

1. Place the diced chicken breasts, chicken broth, chopped carrots, chopped celery, tamari sauce, thyme, and half the parsley into the pressure cooker pot.
2. If you're adding in gelatin, then stir it in until it dissolves.
3. Set the pressure cooker on high pressure for 35 minutes. When ready, follow your pressure cooker's instructions for releasing the pressure safely.
4. Add salt to taste and sprinkle in the rest of the chopped parsley.
5. If you want to thicken the stew, then mix 2 Tablespoons of arrowroot flour in 1/4 cup of cold water and pour the mixture into the broth. Stir and serve immediately.

Chili Topped Parsnip Fries

Prep Time: 10 minutes
Cook Time: 40 minutes
Total Time: 50 minutes
Yield: 2 servings
Serving Size: 1 large bowl *(approx.)*

Jeremy didn't eat many veggies growing up, so he literally never had a parsnip until quite recently. Now, whenever we go to the store, he always heads straight for the parsnips, and it's all because of this recipe. This is one of our most highly-recommended.

INGREDIENTS

- 2 large parsnips *(or 4 small ones)*, peeled and cut into fries
- 1 Tablespoon *(18 g)* salt
- ¼ cup *(60 ml)* olive oil
- 2 14-ounce *(794 g)* cans of tomato sauce or diced tomatoes
- 1 lb *(454 g)* ground beef
- 2 Tablespoons *(30 ml)* coconut oil
- 4 cloves garlic, minced *(or 2-3 Tbsp (17-25 g) garlic powder) (optional)*
- 1 small onion, chopped *(optional)*
- 1 Tablespoon *(5 g)* Italian seasoning
- Salt and pepper to taste
- 4 Tablespoons *(58 g)* of guacamole *(see page 180 for recipe) (optional)*

INSTRUCTIONS

1. Preheat oven to 450 F *(232 C)*.
2. Toss the parsnip fries with 1 Tablespoon of salt and 1/4 cup of olive oil. Spread fries onto a baking tray and bake for 40 minutes *(flip the fries in the middle to prevent burning)*.
3. Meanwhile, add the 2 Tablespoons *(27 g)* coconut oil into a large saucepan and add the ground beef and the onions. Cook the ground beef and onions until the beef is browned. Add the tomato sauce or diced tomatoes, garlic, Italian seasoning, and salt and pepper to taste. Simmer for 30-40 minutes. Stir regularly to keep from burning on the bottom of the pot.
4. Divide the parsnip fries between two bowls. Divide the chili and pour on top of the fries. Then top each bowl with two tablespoons of guacamole.

SUBSTITUTIONS

• Fresh basil leaves can be used instead of Italian seasoning.

Chinese Pork Spare Ribs

Prep Time: 10 minutes
Cook Time: 1 hour 20 minutes
Total Time: 1 hour 30 minutes
Yield: 4 servings
Serving Size: 1 lb (454 g) of ribs

Louise grew up eating a lot of Chinese food cooked by her parents, who are both Chinese. As a consequence, we now make a lot of dishes with spices and flavorings that are Asian-inspired, and these easy ribs are one of our favorites.

INGREDIENTS

- 4 lb *(1.8 kg)* pork spare ribs *(or back ribs)*, chopped into individual ribs
- ½ inch *(1.25 cm)* chunk of fresh ginger, sliced into 2 pieces
- ½ inch *(1.25 cm)* chunk of fresh ginger, finely diced
- ½ cup *(50 g)* scallions *(spring onion, diced), divided into 2 parts*
- 3 star anise *(omit for AIP)*
- 20 Szechuan peppercorns *(omit for AIP)*
- 2 Tablespoons *(36 g)* of salt *(optional)*
- 3 cloves garlic, minced
- 2 Tablespoons *(30 ml)* tamari sauce *(use coconut aminos for AIP)*
- 2 Tablespoons *(30 ml)* of coconut oil, melted

INSTRUCTIONS

1. Place the ribs in a large stockpot filled with water so that the ribs are covered.
2. After the water starts boiling, skim off any foam that forms on the top of the broth *(for prettiness)*.
3. Add the 2 slices of ginger, 1/4 cup of scallions, 3 star anise, the Szechuan peppercorns, and 2 tablespoons of salt to the pot and simmer until the meat is cooked and soft *(approx. 45 minutes)*.
4. Remove the ribs from the pot but keep the broth (pour it through a sieve to remove all solids). The broth *(by itself)* is wonderful to drink with just a bit of salt, or else you can use it as the base for delicious soups.
5. In a small bowl, mix together the diced ginger, rest of the scallions, minced garlic, tamari sauce, and the 2 tablespoons of coconut oil.
6. Heat up a skillet *(or wok if you have one)* on high heat and add the ribs in batches to it. Divide the mixture so that you will have enough for each batch of ribs. Coat each batch of ribs on both sides with the mixture. Double the mixture if you prefer more sauce on the ribs.
7. Sauté the ribs on high heat until they brown and no more liquid remains in the skillet.

SUBSTITUTIONS

- Half an onion, diced, can be used instead of the ½ cup scallions.

Coconut Chicken Curry

Prep Time: 15 minutes
Cook Time: 45 minutes
Total Time: 1 hour
Yield: 2 servings
Serving Size: 1 large bowl

For a while, we didn't eat very much chicken at all. We made a lot of beef and pork dishes, and we forgot how good chicken can be. This recipe reminded us. It's got tons of flavor from the curry sauce, and the chicken stays very moist and tender.

INGREDIENTS

- 3 chicken breasts, cut into chunks
- 1 Tablespoon *(15 ml)* of ghee or coconut oil
- 1 cup *(240 ml)* of coconut cream *(or, alternatively use the top layer of cream from a refrigerated can of coconut milk)*
- 1 cup *(238 ml)* chicken broth
- 2 cups *(256 g)* diced carrots *(for D, use zucchini instead)*
- 1 cup *(101 g)* chopped celery
- 2 tomatoes, diced
- 1½ Tablespoons *(10 g)* curry powder or garam masala
- 1 Tablespoon *(6 g)* grated ginger
- ¼ cup *(4 g)* cilantro, roughly chopped
- 6 cloves garlic, minced
- Salt to taste

INSTRUCTIONS

1. Sauté the chicken in the ghee or coconut oil in a medium-sized saucepan.
2. When the outside of the chicken has all turned white, add in the coconut cream and the chicken broth and mix well.
3. Add in the carrots, celery, and tomatoes.
4. Add in the ginger and curry powder *(or garam masala)*.
5. Cook on medium heat with the lid on for 40 minutes *(stirring occasionally)*.
6. Add in the minced garlic and cilantro and salt to taste. Cook for another 5 minutes and serve.

SUBSTITUTIONS

- Fish or other meats can be used instead of chicken.
- 1 potato, diced, can be used instead of carrots for a thicker curry.
- Garlic powder and ginger powder can be used instead of fresh garlic and ginger.

Fall-off-the-bone BBQ Ribs

Prep Time: 5 minutes
Cook Time: 2 hours
Total Time: 2 hours, 5 minutes
Yield: 2 servings
Serving Size: approx. 6-8 ribs

We still remember the first time we made BBQ ribs. We were living in Oakland, California, and the grill never got very hot. The ribs took 9 hours to cook, but they were so tender and delicious. This recipe won't take you nearly as long, but by boiling the ribs first, you'll achieve the same tenderness faster. We know a lot of people find boiling the ribs odd, but they really do make the ribs very tender!

INGREDIENTS

- 2 lbs *(908 g)* pork spare ribs
- 1 Tablespoon *(18 g)* salt
- 1½ cups *(375 g)* BBQ Sauce *(see page 169 for recipe)*

INSTRUCTIONS

1. Cut the ribs so that they're in slabs of approx. 4 ribs.
2. Place the ribs and salt in a pot of water *(make sure the ribs are submerged in the water)* and boil for 1 hour. If you like, you can use a spoon to remove any scum floating in the water.
3. Preheat oven to 325 F *(163 C)*.
4. Place the boiled ribs in a baking pan and slather a thick layer of BBQ sauce over them *(use approx. 1 cup (250 g) of sauce)*. Place foil over the baking pan and bake for 40 minutes.
5. Remove the foil and bake for another 20 minutes *(you might need to pour more BBQ sauce on if your sauce is very "liquidy" and has run off the ribs)*. [Optional] You can finish the ribs on the grill if you prefer.
6. Serve with additional BBQ sauce if needed.

Fish Sticks

Prep Time: 10 minutes
Cook Time: 20 minutes
Total Time: 30 minutes
Yield: 2 servings
Serving Size: 7-8 fish sticks

We don't have kids, but we know that it can be hard to start feeding your kids a Paleo diet when they're used to eating a lot of processed foods. Plus, we also know how delicious fish sticks are. So we created a version that's both Paleo and amazingly delicious.

INGREDIENTS

- 1 lb *(450 g)* of white fish *(cod, tilapia, haddock)*, chopped into small pieces
- ¼ cup (15g) carrots, shredded
- ¼ cup (40g) onions, finely chopped
- 2 eggs, whisked
- 4 Tablespoons *(28 g)* coconut flour
- 1 Tablespoon *(10g)* arrowroot flour
- 1 Tablespoon *(8 g)* garlic powder
- 1 Tablespoon *(15 ml)* fresh lemon juice
- 1-2 teaspoon *(6-12 g)* salt
- Dash of black pepper
- Coconut oil to cook in
- Ketchup to serve with the fish sticks *(see page 175 for recipe)*

INSTRUCTIONS

1. Add some coconut oil into a skillet and sauté the chopped fish. Don't worry about the fish falling apart. You will know the fish is done once it turns white on the outside and is flaking.
2. After the fish is cooked, flake it well and place it into a large bowl with the carrots, onions, eggs, coconut flour, arrowroot flour, garlic powder, lemon juice, salt, and pepper. Mix well *(can be mixed using your hands)*.
3. Shape the mixture into 13-15 fish sticks.
4. In a skillet on medium heat, add 1 Tablespoon of coconut oil. Cook as many fish sticks as you can fit in the skillet and cook until they turn golden. Turn them over and cook the other side until golden. Repeat until all the fish sticks are cooked *(the fish mixture can fall apart easily before being fully cooked, so be careful when turning them)*.
5. Serve with ketchup *(see page 175 for recipe)*.

Fish Tacos

Prep Time: 30 minutes
Cook Time: 15 minutes
Total Time: 45 minutes
Yield: 2 servings
Serving Size: 2-3 tacos

INGREDIENTS

For the Fish:

- 1 lb *(454 g)* tilapia *(or halibut/cod)*, cut into ½ inch by ¾ inch *(1 cm by 2 cm)* strips
- ½ cup *(56 g)* coconut flour
- 1 Tablespoon *(8 g)* garlic powder
- 2 teaspoons *(12 g)* salt
- 2 teaspoons *(5 g)* cumin powder *(omit for AIP)*
- Coconut oil for frying

For the White Sauce: *(omit for AIP)*

- ½ cup *(120 g)* mayo *(see page 172 for recipe)*
- 1 Tablespoon *(15 ml)* lime juice
- 1 teaspoon *(2 g)* dried oregano
- ½ teaspoon *(1 g)* cumin powder
- Dash of chili powder
- ½ teaspoon *(4 g)* of raw honey *(optional)*

To Eat:

- 4-6 lettuce leaves
- 1 cup salsa *(omit for AIP)*
- 2 Tablespoons *(2 g)* cilantro, chopped
- 4-6 slices of lime

INSTRUCTIONS

For the White Sauce:

1. Mix all ingredients together with a fork. Add in the honey if you find the sauce too sour.

For the Fish:

2. Mix together all dry ingredients *(coconut flour, garlic powder, cumin powder, salt, & pepper)* in a bowl.
3. Drop the fish strips into the bowl and coat with the coconut flour mixture.
4. Heat up enough coconut oil in a saucepan so that the coconut oil is approx. 1/2 inch (1-2 cm) deep. Use a high heat.
5. Carefully add the coated fish strips to the hot coconut oil.
6. Fry until the coconut flour coating turns a golden brown color *(takes approx. 5 minutes)*. You should turn the fish strips over after a few minutes since the oil doesn't cover the entire piece of fish.
7. Place the fried fish strips in a bowl lined with a paper towel to soak up the excess oil.

To Eat:

8. Wash the lettuce leaves and pat dry with a paper towel.
9. Place 5-6 fish strips onto of a lettuce leaf. Top with salsa and white sauce. Sprinkle some chopped cilantro on top for garnish and serve with a few slices of lime.

SUBSTITUTIONS

- The white sauce can be omitted.
- Collard greens or other Paleo wraps can be used instead of lettuce leaves.

Spinach Basil Chicken Meatballs with Plum Balsamic Sauce

Prep Time: 10 minutes
Cook Time: 15 minutes
Total Time: 25 minutes
Yield: 2 servings
Serving Size: 20-24 meatballs

These are great as an appetizer or as an entree, and the plum balsamic sauce goes really well with the meatballs. This dish is also a fantastic way to get more spinach into your diet.

INGREDIENTS

For the Meatballs:
- 2 chicken breasts *(approx. 1 lb or 450 g)*
- ¼ lb *(115 g)* spinach
- 2 teaspoons *(12 g)* salt
- 10 basil leaves
- 5 cloves of garlic, peeled
- 3 Tablespoons *(44 ml)* olive oil
- 2 Tablespoons *(30 ml)* olive oil or avocado oil to cook in

For the Plum Balsamic Sauce:
- 2 plums, pitted
- ½ Tablespoon *(8 ml)* balsamic vinegar
- ½ Tablespoon *(11 g)* of raw honey
- 2 Tablespoons *(32 ml)* water

INSTRUCTIONS

1. Place the chicken breasts, spinach, salt, basil leaves, garlic, and 3 Tablespoons of olive oil into a food processor and process well.
2. Make ping-pong sized meatballs from the meat mixture.
3. Add the 2 Tablespoons olive oil or avocado oil to a frying pan and fry the meatballs for 5 minutes on medium heat (fry in 2 batches if necessary). Turn the meatballs and fry for another 10 minutes. Make sure the meatballs don't get burnt.
4. Meanwhile make the plum balsamic sauce - place the pitted plums, balsamic vinegar, raw honey, and water into a blender and blend well.
5. Pour half the sauce into the frying pan with the meatballs and turn up the heat. Brown the meatballs in the sauce - keep turning the meatballs in the sauce until the sauce is gone and the meatballs are brown.
6. Check the meatballs are fully cooked by cutting into one or using a meat thermometer. Serve with the rest of the plum balsamic sauce.

Guacamole Burger

Prep Time: 10 minutes
Cooking Time: 20 minutes
Total Time: 30 minutes
Yield: 4 servings
Serving Size: 1 burger

We make these burgers all the time. It's another super-simple recipe, but it's important, because these guacamole burgers make you forget all about the buns and condiments that you're not eating any longer. Don't underestimate this type of recipe just because it's simple!

INGREDIENTS

- 1-1½ lbs *(454-731 g)* ground beef
- 4 eggs *(use bacon slices or lettuce for AIP)*
- 1 cup *(232 g)* guacamole *(see page 180 for recipe) (use just avocados for AIP)*

INSTRUCTIONS

1. With your hands, mold the ground beef into 4 patties.
2. Cook the 4 burger patties, either in a skillet with a bit of coconut oil or on a grill. Ensure that the skillet/grill is very hot before placing the burger patties on, and flip the patties just once.
3. Once the burgers are cooked through, place to the side.
4. Fry the eggs *(preferably in coconut oil)* in a skillet.
5. Place 1 fried egg on top of each burger and then top with guacamole *(see page 180 for recipe)*.

SUBSTITUTIONS

- Store-bought guacamole can be used instead of making it yourself *(check ingredients first!)*.
- You can cook the burgers in advance in a large batch and just heat up during the week.

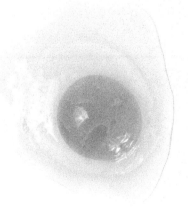

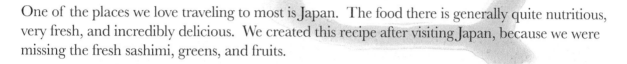

Mango Sashimi Salad

Prep Time: 15 minutes
Cook Time: 0 minutes
Total Time: 15 minutes
Yield: 2 servings
Serving Size: 1 bowl

One of the places we love traveling to most is Japan. The food there is generally quite nutritious, very fresh, and incredibly delicious. We created this recipe after visiting Japan, because we were missing the fresh sashimi, greens, and fruits.

INGREDIENTS

- 2 handfuls of baby kale leaves
- 1 Ataulfo mango, peeled and sliced
- ½ lb *(227 g)* salmon sashimi, sliced into 10-12 slices
- ½ Tablespoon *(11 g)* raw honey
- 3 Tablespoons *(45 ml)* tamari sauce *(use coconut aminos for AIP)*
- 2 Tablespoons *(30 ml)* olive oil
- 1 teaspoon *(5 ml)* balsamic vinegar

INSTRUCTIONS

1. In a small bowl, mix together the honey, tamari sauce, olive oil, and balsamic vinegar to make the salad dressing.
2. Toss the dressing with kale leaves in a large bowl, and then divide into 2 bowls.
3. Top each bowl of salad with mango slices and sashimi.

SUBSTITUTIONS

• Other salad leaves can be used instead of baby kale leaves.
• Smoked salmon can be used instead of salmon sashimi *(but make the honey mustard dressing (see page 174 for recipe) instead of the tamari dressing described on this page).*
• Other types of mangos can be used *(texture may not be as soft).*

Marinated Grilled Flank Steak

Prep Time: 8 hours *(for marinating)*
Cook Time: 30 minutes
Total Time: 8 hours 30 minutes
Yield: 4 servings
Serving Size: 8-12 oz steak

Flank steak is one of our favorite cuts of beef, but if you're not careful, it can get a bit tough and chewy. A good marinade helps with this, but if you're in a hurry, this dish still tastes great with just 1 hour of marinating.

INGREDIENTS

- 3 lbs *(1361 g)* flank steak
- 1 cup *(240 ml)* olive oil
- 2/3 cup *(160 ml)* tamari sauce *(use coconut aminos for AIP)*
- ½ cup *(120 ml)* apple cider vinegar
- Juice from 1 lemon
- 2 Tablespoons *(28 g)* of yellow mustard *(omit for AIP)*
- 6 cloves of garlic, crushed
- 1 Tablespoon *(5 g)* grated ginger *(or ginger powder)*
- 1 Tablespoon *(5 g)* paprika *(omit for AIP)*
- 1 Tablespoon *(6 g)* onion powder
- 1 Tablespoon *(18 g)* salt
- 2 teaspoons *(3 g)* dried thyme
- 1 teaspoon *(3 g)* chili powder *(omit for AIP)*

INSTRUCTIONS

1. Cut the flank steak into manageable pieces if it's not already cut so.
2. Create the marinade by mixing all ingredients *(except the steak)* in a small bowl.
3. Place each piece of steak into a Ziploc bag and divide the marinade equally among the bags.
4. Seal the bags and marinate the steak overnight.
5. When ready, grill each steak by placing on a hot grill or skillet. Try to turn the steaks as little as possible. You can use a meat thermometer to get the steak to the level of rareness you desire. *(We found 3-4 minutes on each side on a hot 500-600 F grill with the lid down worked well.)*

SUBSTITUTIONS

- Many of the spices can be changed up or omitted for different flavors.

Orange Beef Stirfry

Prep Time: 15 minutes
Cook Time: 15 minutes
Total Time: 30 minutes
Yield: 2 servings
Serving Size: 1 plate

Orange chicken is a popular dish in the US, but did you know that orange beef is also delicious?
Try this dish with some cauliflower white "rice" for a Chinese-style Paleo dinner.

INGREDIENTS

- ½ lb *(225 g)* beef round, sliced into thin slices (1-inch in length)
- 2 small oranges, chopped
- 2 cloves garlic, minced
- 1 teaspoon freshly grated ginger (optional)
- 2 Tablespoons *(30 ml)* tamari sauce *(use coconut aminos for AIP)*
- 2 Tablespoons chopped green onions (scallions)
- 1 Tablespoon *(15 ml)* coconut oil or avocado oil to cook in
- 1 Tablespoon cilantro, chopped (for garnish)
- Salt to taste

INSTRUCTIONS

1. Place the coconut or avocado oil into a skillet or wok or frying pan. Add in the scallions and then the beef slices and sauté on high heat until most of the beef has turned brown.

2. Add in the oranges, garlic, ginger, tamari sauce and saute on high for 2-3 minutes more until the beef is fully cooked.

3. Add salt to taste, garnish with cilantro, and serve.

SUBSTITUTIONS

- 1/4 onion (chopped) can be used instead of the scallions.
- Chicken can be used instead of beef.

Mu Shu Pork

Prep Time: 15 minutes
Cook Time: 15 minutes
Total Time: 30 minutes
Yield: 2 servings
Serving Size: 1 bowl

This is another recipe that Louise thought up one day when we had a lot of pork and Napa cabbage lying around. Oddly enough, we can't remember if we'd ever had Mu Shu Pork *(even the non-Paleo versions)* before.

INGREDIENTS

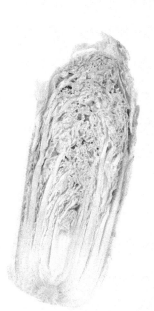

- ½ lb *(227 g)* pork tenderloin, cut into small thin 1-inch long str···
- 3 eggs, whisked *(omit for AIP)*
- 15 Napa cabbage leaves, chopped into thin strips
- 1 cup *(89 g)* shiitake mushrooms, sliced
- 1 8-ounce *(227 g)* can of sliced bamboo shoots
- ½ teaspoon *(1 g)* freshly grated ginger
- 1 Tablespoon *(15 ml)* tamari sauce *(use coconut aminos for AIP)*
- ½ teaspoon *(2.5 ml)* apple cider vinegar
- Salt to taste
- 1 Tablespoon + 1 teaspoon *(18 ml total)* coconut oil to cook in
- ¼ cup *(25 g)* scallions *(for garnish)*
- Lettuce leaves to serve pork in *(optional)*

INSTRUCTIONS

1. Add 1 Tablespoon *(14 g)* of coconut oil to a skillet on medium heat.
2. Add a little bit of salt to the whisked eggs and pour the mixture into the skillet. Let it cook undisturbed into a pancake. Flip the egg pancake once it's cooked most of the way through *(it needs to be fairly solid when you flip it)*. Cook for a few more minutes, then place on a cutting board and cut into thin 1-inch long strips.
3. Cook the pork in a teaspoon of coconut oil. Stir with a spatula to make sure the strips don't clump together.
4. Once the pork is cooked, add in the strips of eggs, sliced mushrooms, sliced Napa cabbage, and bamboo shoots. Add in the ginger, tamari sauce, and apple cider vinegar.
5. Cook until the cabbage and mushrooms are soft. Then add salt to taste.
6. Sprinkle the scallions on top for garnish and serve dish in lettuce cups or by itself.

SUBSTITUTIONS

- Bamboo shoots can be omitted or sliced asparagus can be used instead.

Pressure Cooker Jamaican Oxtail Stew

Prep Time: 15 minutes
Cook Time: 50 minutes
Total Time: 1 hour 5 minutes
Yield: 4 servings
Serving Size: 1 large bowl

This Jamaican oxtail stew is traditionally made with beans, and so I've replaced the beans with whole almonds (which you can omit for a nut-free version). If you don't have a pressure cooker, you can make this dish in the slow cooker - put it on the low setting for 8-10 hours and add more water so that it covers the meat. The meat should almost be falling off the bone when done.

INGREDIENTS

- 2 lb *(900 g)* oxtail
- ½ large onion, chopped
- 2 green onions, chopped
- 6 cloves garlic, peeled
- 2 Tablespoons ginger, minced
- ¼ cup *(60 ml)* tamari sauce *(use coconut aminos for AIP)*
- 1 sprig thyme
- 1 chili pepper *(omit for AIP)*
- ¼ cup *(40 g)* whole almonds *(omit for AIP)*
- Salt and pepper to taste *(omit pepper for AIP)*
- 2 cups *(500 ml)* water
- 2 Tablespoons *(30 ml)* avocado oil to cook with

INSTRUCTIONS

1. Place the avocado oil into a frying pan and add the chopped onions and oxtail. Cook the onions and oxtail on high heat until the outside of the oxtail starts to brown (approx. 5-10 minutes). Stir regularly.

2. Place the browned oxtail and onions along with all the other ingredients into the pressure cooker.

3. Cook on high pressure for 50 minutes. When ready, follow your pressure cooker's instructions for releasing the pressure safely.

No-Pastry Beef Wellington

Prep Time: 30 minutes
Cook Time: 30 minutes
Total Time: 60 minutes
Yield: 2 servings
Serving Size: ½ of a Beef Wellington

We're both big fans of Gordon Ramsay. We've been to several of his restaurants, and we generally think (notwithstanding his television persona) that he's a great chef. Among the dishes he's known for is his Beef Wellington. Our version isn't really like his *(it has no pastry after all)*, but it's delicious anyway.

INGREDIENTS

For the Duxelles:
- 3 large button mushrooms
- 1 Tablespoon *(10 g)* onions, chopped
- 1 teaspoon *(3 g)* garlic powder
- 1/2 teaspoon (3g) salt
- 2 Tablespoons *(30 ml)* olive oil

Other Ingredients:
- 1 9-ounce *(255 g)* filet mignon
- 8 thin slices of prosciutto *(or 4 slices ham)*
- 1 Tablespoon *(14 g)* yellow mustard *(omit for AIP)*
- ½ Tablespoon *(9 g)* salt
- 2 Tablespoons *(30 ml)* olive oil to cook in

INSTRUCTIONS

1. Preheat oven to 400 F *(204 C)*.
2. Make the Duxelles by blending the mushrooms, onions, garlic, salt, and olive oil together until pureed.
3. Then heat the mixture in a pan for 10 minutes on medium heat.
4. Place a large piece of cling-film onto the counter and place the pieces of prosciutto side-by-side *(overlapping slightly)* to form a rectangular layer.
5. Spread the duxelles over the prosciutto layer.
6. Sprinkle the ½ Tablespoon of salt over the filet mignon.
7. Pan-sear the filet mignon in 2 Tablespoons of olive oil.
8. Spread the 1 Tablespoon of mustard on the seared filet mignon and place in the middle of the prosciutto and duxelles layer.
9. Use the cling-film to wrap the prosciutto around the filet mignon. Then wrap the cling-film around the package to secure it. Use a second piece of cling-film to pull the prosciutto-wrapped package tighter together. Placc in fridge for 15 minutes.
10. Remove the cling-film from the refrigerated prosciutto-wrapped beef and place on a greased baking tray.
11. Bake for 20-25 minutes *(it should be pink when you cut into it)*.
12. To serve, carefully cut the Beef Wellington in half.

Old Fashioned Lasagna

Prep Time: 15 minutes
Cook Time: 1 hour 50 minutes
Total Time: 2 hours 5 minutes
Yield: 8 servings
Serving Size: 1 large slice

Back when Louise was in law school, we used to throw regular dinner parties for our friends. *(Jeremy has always loved hosting and planning events.)* Our most popular dish was our lasagna, but at some point, we refused to eat pasta any longer. As a result, we were forced to come up with this recipe, which is, perhaps, better than the "normal" version.

INGREDIENTS

- ¾ lb *(341 g)* ground pork *(or use meat of your choice)*
- ¾ lb *(341 g)* ground beef *(or use meat of your choice)*
- 1 small onion, minced
- 1 28-ounce *(794 g)* can diced or crushed tomatoes
- 2 6-ounce *(170 g)* cans of tomato paste
- 2 Tablespoons *(5 g)* fresh basil, finely chopped
- 6 Tablespoons *(23 g)* fresh parsley, finely chopped
- 1 Tablespoon *(3 g)* fresh oregano, finely chopped
- 1 Tablespoon *(3 g)* fresh thyme, finely chopped
- 1 teaspoon *(2 g)* fennel seeds
- 4 cloves garlic, crushed
- 2 eggs, whisked
- 2 Tablespoons *(30 ml)* coconut oil
- Salt to taste
- 1 large eggplant *(or 2 Japanese eggplants)*, sliced into thin slices
- 3 eggs for topping *(optional)*
- 3 Tablespoons *(54 g)* salt for boiling eggplants

INSTRUCTIONS

1. Place 2 Tablespoons of coconut oil into a large stock pot. Add in the ground meat and the minced onion. Cook until the meat browns and the onion turns translucent.
2. Then add in the tomatoes, tomato paste, fresh herbs, fennel seeds, and crushed garlic.
3. Cook on a low simmer with the lid on for 45 minutes. Stir regularly to make sure nothing sticks to the bottom of the pot.
4. Preheat the oven to 375 F *(191 C)* and boil a pot of water. Add the 3 Tablespoons of salt into the boiling water, then add in the eggplant slices. Boil for 2-3 minutes and then remove and place in cold water *(if your slices are thicker, then you might need to boil for longer - the eggplant should soften so that you can cut it with a fork fairly easily)*.
5. Add the whisked eggs into the meat mixture and stir slowly to mix the eggs in. Cook the meat mixture for 10 minutes more and then add salt to taste.
6. Pour half the meat mixture into the bottom of a 13 by 9 inch lasagna pan or a similar baking pan. Top with half the eggplant slices.
7. Then pour the other half of the egg/meat mixture on top of the eggplant slices, and top that egg/meat layer with the rest of the eggplant slices.
8. Cover the tray with aluminum foil and bake for 30 minutes.
9. Remove the foil and crack the 3 eggs on top *(optional)*. Bake for 15-20 more minutes until the egg whites become solid.

SUBSTITUTIONS

- Fresh tomatoes can be used instead of canned tomatoes.
- Dried herbs can be used instead of fresh herbs.

Thai Chicken Pad See Ew

Prep Time: 10 minutes
Cook Time: 15 minutes
Total Time: 25 minutes
Yield: 2 servings
Serving Size: 1 large plate

Pad see ew (AKA chicken and broccoli stir-fried with flat rice noodles) is one of our favorite Thai dishes, and you'll find it on the menu at most Thai restaurants. While white rice and rice noodles are something we are sometimes OK with eating when traveling (white rice is often considered a clean starch), it's still something we try to avoid when at home, so this recipe uses easy cucumber noodles instead. Use a potato peeler to create your cucumber noodles!

INGREDIENTS

- 1 chicken breast *(0.5 lb or 250 g)*, cut into small, thin pieces
- ¼ cup *(0.6 oz or 17 g)* green onion, diced (scallions)
- 1 cup *(4 oz or 115 g)* broccoli florets, broken into small florets
- 1 teaspoon freshly grated ginger
- 1 Tablespoon *(15 ml)* tamari sauce *(use coconut aminos for AIP)*
- 2 cloves garlic, minced
- 1 Tablespoon cilantro, finely chopped
- 1 Tablespoon *(15 ml)* coconut oil to cook in
- 1 cucumber, peeled into long noodles using a potato peeler
- Salt to taste

INSTRUCTIONS

1. Add 1 Tablespoon of coconut oil into a large saucepan, and sauté the chicken breast and green onions in it.
2. Add in the broccoli, ginger, and tamari sauce. Place a lid over the saucepan and let the broccoli cook on medium heat until it's tender to your liking (approx. 5-10 minutes). Stir regularly.
3. Meanwhile, peel the cucumber and then create the cucumber noodles by using a potato peeler to peel the cucumber into long, wide strands. Divide the cucumber noodles between two plates.
4. Add to the saucepan the minced garlic, cilantro, and salt to taste. Serve on top of the cucumber noodles.

Oven Braised Boneless Short Ribs

Prep Time: 15 minutes
Cook Time: 50 minutes
Total Time: 1 hour 5 minutes
Yield: 6-8 servings
Serving Size: 1 cup (approx.)

This is a recipe that we use at least a couple times per month. The reason we use it so often is because once you've prepared these ribs, you can refrigerate and eat them by themselves, or you can shred/slice the meat and use it in a variety of other dishes. We are all about cooking once and then having food available for several days, and this recipe makes that very easy.

INGREDIENTS

- 6-7 boneless beef short ribs
- 2 Tablespoons *(30 ml)* white wine *(or vodka)*
- ½ cup *(118 ml)* tamari sauce
- ¼ large onion, diced
- 2 cloves garlic, crushed
- 20 Szechuan peppercorns
- 2 Tablespoons (8 g) parsley, finely chopped
- ½ teaspoon *(1 g)* black pepper

INSTRUCTIONS

1. Preheat oven to 375 F *(191 C)*.
2. Place the beef short ribs into a large pot of water and bring to the boil for 5 minutes.
3. In a small bowl, mix together the white wine, tamari sauce, diced onions, garlic, peppercorns, parsley, and black pepper. This is the sauce.
4. Place the short ribs onto a small baking tray – pack it as tightly as possible without placing any on top of each other.
5. Pour the sauce over the short ribs in the baking tray so that the short ribs are now sitting in the sauce. The idea is to have ½-inch *(1.25 cm)* of sauce at the bottom of the baking tray, which will be cooked off during the baking process.
6. Loosely cover the baking tray with foil and bake for 20 minutes. Turn the boneless short ribs over so the other side gets some of the sauce. Bake for another 20 minutes.
7. Then remove the foil and bake for 10 more minutes until the sauce is mostly gone.
8. Serve immediately or store for use in other dishes *(e.g, the Sweet Potato Breakfast Hash)*.

SUBSTITUTIONS

- For an easier dish, omit the onion, garlic, peppercorns, parsley, and black pepper.

Peach and Steak Salad

Prep Time: 10 minutes
Cook Time: 20 minutes (to cook the steak)
Total Time: 30 minutes
Yield: 2 servings
Serving Size: 1 bowl

As you probably noticed from a few of our recipes *(Pork and Pineapple, Orange Beef Stirfry, Raspberry Chili, etc.)*, we really like combining fruits with our meats. It's something we've learned along the way that really makes various dishes stand out.

INGREDIENTS

- 2 peaches
- 1 head of romaine lettuce
- Handful of baby kale leaves
- 2 6-ounce *(170 g)* steaks, grilled or pan-fried *(or used the short-ribs - recipe on page 97)*
- 3 Tablespoons (45 ml) olive oil
- 1 Tablespoon *(15 ml)* balsamic vinegar

INSTRUCTIONS

1. Dice the peaches and the cooked steaks.
2. Toss the peach, steak, romaine lettuce, and kale leaves with the olive oil and balsamic vinegar.

SUBSTITUTIONS

- Nectarines, apricots, or pears can be used instead of peaches.
- Other salad greens can be used instead of romaine lettuce and baby kale leaves.

Pineapple Pork

Prep Time: 5 minutes
Cook Time: 10 minutes
Total Time: 15 minutes
Yield: 2 servings
Serving Size: 1 medium bowl

If you've been following us for any length of time *(or if you've seen many of Jeremy's videos)*, then you probably know that this is his absolute favorite recipe. Part of that is because he's lazy and loves how fast this dish can be prepared. Another part of it is because it's just so yummy.

INGREDIENTS

- 2 cups *(490 g)* of pineapple chunks *(frozen or fresh)*
- 3 cups *(747 g)* of shredded pork *(see page 124 for recipe)*
- 1 teaspoon *(2 g)* of freshly grated ginger
- 3 cloves of garlic, minced
- ¼ cup *(4 g)* of cilantro, chopped
- Salt to taste
- 1 Tablespoon *(15 ml)* coconut oil to cook in

INSTRUCTIONS

1. Melt 1 tablespoon of coconut oil in a saucepan and add in the pineapple chunks. Cook until softened.
2. Add in the shredded pork and cook for 5 minutes.
3. Add in the ginger, garlic, cilantro, and season with salt to taste.

SUBSTITUTIONS

- Cilantro and ginger can be omitted.
- Garlic powder can be used instead of fresh garlic.

Popcorn Shrimp

Prep Time: 5 minutes
Cook Time: 20 minutes
Total Time: 25 minutes
Yield: 2 servings
Serving Size: ¼ lb (113 g) shrimp

Jeremy ate pretty much zero seafood growing up, except for popcorn shrimp. Recently, we wanted to try recreating some of the dishes we used to love as kids, and since this was one of Jeremy's favorites, we tried it. You (and your kids if you have them) are not going to be disappointed.

INGREDIENTS

- ½ lb *(227 g)* of small shrimp, peeled
- 2 eggs, beaten
- 6 Tablespoons *(26 g)* of cajun seasoning *(see page 171 for recipe)*
- 6 Tablespoons *(42 g)* of coconut flour
- Coconut oil for frying

INSTRUCTIONS

1. Melt the coconut oil in a saucepan (use enough coconut oil so that it's ½ inch *(1-2 cm)* deep) or deep fryer.
2. Place the beaten eggs into one large bowl, and in another large bowl, combine the coconut flour and seasoning.
3. Drop a handful of the shrimp into the beaten eggs and stir around so that each shrimp is coated.
4. Then take the shrimp from the beaten eggs and place into the seasoning bowl. Coat the shrimp with the coconut flour and seasoning mixture.
5. Place the coated shrimp into the oil and fry until golden. Try not to stir the pot and don't place too many shrimp into the pot at once *(make sure all the shrimp is touching the oil)*.
6. Using a slotted spoon, remove the shrimp and place on paper towels to absorb the excess oil. Repeat for the rest of the shrimp (change the oil if there are too many solids in it).
7. Cool for 10 minutes *(the outside will get crisp)* and enjoy by itself or with some ketchup *(see page 175 for recipe)*.

Italian Seasoning Crusted Lamb

Prep Time: 5 minutes
Cook Time: 30 minutes
Total Time: 35 minutes
Yield: 1 serving
Serving Size: 1 lamb steak

This is such an easy way to cook flavorful and tender lamb steaks or lamb chops. The instructions are for baking in the oven, but you can also put this on the grill. It's easy to double, triple, etc. this recipe and it works equally well with lamb steaks as well as lamb chops - just adjust the cooking time depending on the thickness of the lamb.

INGREDIENTS

- 1 lamb steak or chop *(0.5 lb or 250 g) (approx. 3/4-inch thick)*
- 1 Tablespoon *(0.3 oz or 9 g)* Italian seasoning
- 2 Tablespoons *(0.6 oz or 17 g)* garlic powder
- Salt to taste

INSTRUCTIONS

1. Preheat oven to 375 F (190 C).
2. Combine the Italian seasoning, garlic powder, and salt. Taste the mixture and adjust to taste.
3. Dip each lamb steak (or lamb chop) into the mixture and coat well.
4. Place on a baking tray and cook in the oven for 15 minutes. Then flip the lamb steak/chop and cook for another 15 minutes. This gets the lamb to around medium to medium well. Decrease or increase the cooking time for thinner or thicker steaks/chops or if you like your lamb rare or well done.

SUBSTITUTION

- Curry powder or cumin powder can be used instead of Italian seasoning for a different flavor.

Tamari Honey Glazed Chicken Drumsticks

Prep Time: 10 minutes
Cook Time: 30 minutes
Total Time: 40 minutes
Yield: 4 servings
Serving Size: 2 drumsticks

This dish combines a lot of flavors - salty with sweet with sour - which makes it very tasty. Plus of course, it's really easy to make!

INGREDIENTS

- 8 chicken drumsticks
- 3 Tablespoons *(54 g)* salt
- 1½ Tablespoons *(32 g)* raw honey
- ½ cup *(120 ml)* tamari sauce *(use coconut aminos for AIP)*
- Juice from 1 lime

INSTRUCTIONS

1. Preheat oven to 400 F (205 C).
2. Dissolve the salt into a pot of cold water. Place the chicken drumsticks in the salted water and bring to the boil - then boil for 5 minutes.
3. Make the tamari honey sauce by mixing together the honey, tamari sauce, and lime juice. Save ¼ of the sauce for serving.
4. Coat the boiled chicken drumsticks in the tamari honey sauce and place on a baking tray.
5. Bake for 10 minutes and then brush extra sauce onto the drumsticks and turn them.
6. Bake for 10-20 more minutes until skin becomes crispier.
7. Drizzle the sauce you saved onto the drumsticks and serve.

Red Wine Beef Bacon Stew *(Bourguignon)*

Prep Time: 10 minutes
Cook Time: 2 hour, 10 minutes
Total Time: 2 hour, 20 minutes
Servings: 4 servings
Yield: 1 large bowl

We've never claimed to be master-chefs. We've been to a lot of the best restaurants in the world, and we've seen what great chefs are capable of. However, if you want a good approximation of a traditionally great French dish, this is it. We love Beef Bourguignon, and with the major exception of the flour added to the broth, it's already pretty Paleo.

INGREDIENTS

- 2 lbs *(908 g)* beef stew meat
- 6 medium carrots, peeled and roughly chopped *(decrease amount for D)*
- ½ lb *(227 g)* green beans *(use celery for AIP)*
- ½ pound *(227 g)* thick cut bacon, cooked and diced
- 8-12 cups *(1.9-2.8 l)* water or broth (so it covers all the meat and vegetables)
- 3 Tablespoons *(21 g)* unflavored gelatin *(optional)*
- 3 Tablespoons *(18 g)* cumin powder *(omit for AIP)*
- 3 Tablespoons *(15 g)* dried onion flakes *(or substitute 1 chopped onion or onion powder)*
- 1 Tablespoon *(7 g)* turmeric
- 1 Tablespoon (8 g) garlic powder *(or substitute 3 cloves of garlic, minced)*
- 1 teaspoon *(2 g)* ginger powder *(or substitute 1 freshly teaspoon grated ginger)*
- 1 cup *(240 ml)* red wine *(omit for AIP)*
- Salt to taste

INSTRUCTIONS

1. Add the beef, carrots, and green beans to the 8-12 cups (1.9-2.8 l) of water or broth in a large pot and bring to a boil. Then add in the gelatin and the spices and mix well. Place the lid on the pot and let simmer for 1 hour (simmer for 2 hours if you have time). Stir to make sure it doesn't stick to the bottom.
2. When the vegetables are soft, add in the cooked pieces of bacon and the red wine.
3. Simmer for 5-10 minutes more.

SUBSTITUTIONS

• Parsnips or baby carrots can be used instead of carrots, celery or Brussel sprouts can be used instead of green beans, and gelatin and red wine can be omitted.

Rosemary Baked Salmon

Prep Time: 5 minutes
Cook Time: 30 minutes
Total Time: 35 minutes
Yield: 2 servings
Serving Size: 1 filet

Another recipe that we eat all the time. You can even use frozen salmon for this one *(although fresh is always a little tastier)*.

INGREDIENTS

- 2 salmon fillets *(fresh or defrosted)*
- 1 Tablespoon (2 g) fresh rosemary leaves
- ¼ cup *(60 ml)* olive oil
- 1 teaspoon *(6 g)* salt *(optional or to taste)*

INSTRUCTIONS

1. Preheat the oven to 350 F *(177 C)*.
2. Mix the olive oil, rosemary, and salt together in a bowl.
3. Place one salmon fillet at a time into the mixture and rub the mixture onto the fillet.
4. Wrap each fillet in a piece of aluminum foil with some of the remaining mixture.
5. Bake for 25-30 minutes.

SUBSTITUTIONS

- Fresh or dried dill can be used instead of the rosemary leaves *(dried rosemary can also be used)*.

Slow Cooker Bacon & Chicken

Prep Time: 10 minutes
Cook Time: 8 hours
Total Time: 8 hours 10 minutes
Yield: 4-6 servings
Serving Size: 1 plate

Bacon obviously makes just about everything better, and chicken is no exception. Chicken - because it's low in fat - can often get a bit dry, especially when you put it in a slow cooker. Adding the bacon to the recipe allows the chicken to stay moister and also allows you to eat more bacon. Win-Win.

INGREDIENTS

- 5 chicken breasts
- 10 sliccs of bacon
- 2 Tablespoons *(9 g)* thyme *(dried)*
- 1 Tablespoon *(5 g)* oregano *(dried)*
- 1 Tablespoon *(3 g)* rosemary *(dried)*
- 5 Tablespoons *(75 ml)* olive oil *(2 Tbsp (30 ml) for the slow cooker and 3 Tbsp (45 ml) after cooking)*
- 1 Tablespoon *(18 g)* salt

INSTRUCTIONS

1. Place all the ingredients into a slow cooker pot and mix together.
2. Cook on the low temperature setting for 8 hours.
3. Shred the meat and mix with 3 tablespoons of olive oil.

SUBSTITUTIONS

- Italian seasoning can be used instead of the thyme, oregano, and rosemary.

Slow Cooker Beef Stew

Prep Time: 10 minutes
Cook Time: 8 hours
Total Time: 8 hours, 10 minutes
Yield: 4-6 servings
Serving Size: 1 bowl

The reason we have so many slow cooker recipes in this cookbook is because they make your life and diet so much easier. We absolutely love putting something in at night, having it ready the next day to eat, and then having leftovers that we can eat for several days later. We know that many folks don't love eating leftovers, and Louise understands that better than anybody, but when it comes down to being able to stick to a great diet, leftovers often play a hugely important role.

INGREDIENTS

- 2.5 lbs *(1.1 kg)* beef *(stew meat or short ribs meat)*
- 4 carrots
- 2 white parsnips
- 2 sweet potatoes
- 1 small onion
- 4 celery sticks
- 2 cloves of garlic, minced
- 1 14.5-ounce *(420 ml)* can of broth *(beef, chicken, or vegetable)*
- 2 teaspoons *(12 g)* salt
- ½ teaspoon *(1 g)* black pepper *(omit for AIP)*
- 1 teaspoon *(3 g)* garlic powder
- 1 teaspoon *(2 g)* onion powder
- 2 teaspoons *(4 g)* paprika *(omit for AIP)*

INSTRUCTIONS

1. Chop up the beef into 1-inch *(2.5 cm)* cubes if you're not using stew meat.
2. Pour the broth into the bottom of the slow cooker.
3. Place the meat into the slow cooker.
4. Season the meat in the slow cooker with salt, pepper, garlic powder, onion powder, minced garlic and paprika.
5. Chop up the vegetables into rough 1-inch *(2.5 cm)* cubes and place on top of the meat in the slow cooker.
6. Place the lid on the slow cooker and cook on the low temperature setting for 8 hours.

SUBSTITUTIONS

- Lamb, chicken, or turkey can be used instead of beef.
- Other vegetables can be used.

Slow Cooker Jerk Chicken

Prep Time: 10 minutes
Cook Time: 5 hours
Total Time: 5 hours, 10 minutes
Yield: 4 servings
Serving Size: 2-3 pieces of chicken

We visited Jamaica a few years ago. It's an amazing place, and the food is spectacular. In particular, their jerk chicken is mouth-watering. And whenever we find a mouth-watering dish, we're always determined to re-create it.

INGREDIENTS

- 5 chicken drumsticks and 5 chicken wings *(or you can use a whole chicken or 5 chicken breasts)*
- 4 teaspoons *(24 g)* salt
- 4 teaspoons *(9 g)* paprika
- 1 teaspoon *(2 g)* cayenne pepper
- 2 teaspoons *(5 g)* onion powder
- 2 teaspoons *(3 g)* dried thyme
- 2 teaspoons *(4 g)* white pepper
- 2 teaspoons *(6 g)* garlic powder
- 1 teaspoons *(2 g)* black pepper

INSTRUCTIONS

1. Mix all the spices together in a bowl to make a rub for the chicken. If you don't want your chicken to be spicy, then leave out the cayenne pepper and instead add in more onion powder, but note that the paprika will still make it slightly spicy.
2. Wash the chicken meat in cold water briefly. Place the washed chicken meat into the bowl with the rub, and rub the spices onto the meat thoroughly – try to get it under the chicken skin if you can. The wings and drumsticks work well here because you can rub the spices under the skin easily.
3. Place each piece of chicken covered with the spices into the slow cooker *(no liquid required)*.
4. Set the slow cooker on medium or low heat *(325 F (163 C) if your slow cooker has a temperature controller)*, and cook for 5-6 hours or until the chicken meat falls off the bone *(slow cooker times can vary dramatically - increase the time if the meat doesn't seem to be falling off the bone)*.
5. You can serve the chicken with the bone on or take the bones out since the meat falls off so easily.

SUBSTITUTIONS

- You can omit the salt initially and add salt to taste when serving.
- Extra black pepper can be used instead of white pepper.

Slow Cooker Raspberry Chili

Prep Time: 15 minutes
Cook Time: 8 hours
Total Time: 8 hours 15 minutes
Yield: 6+ servings

Serving Size: 1 small bowl

We love chili, but one thing that we really love about this recipe is that it's a very easy way to get more liver into your diet. And at least as importantly, you can serve this to people *(or children)* who'd normally never eat liver. If you don't tell them there's liver in it, they'll likely never notice.

INGREDIENTS

- 3 lbs *(1361 g)* ground or minced beef
- 1 lb *(454 g)* ground liver *(optional, but recommended)*
- 3 14.5-ounce *(411 g)* cans diced tomatoes
- 2 6-ounce *(170 g)* cans tomato paste
- 1 lb *(454 g)* raspberries
- 2 bell peppers, diced
- 2 chili peppers, deseeded and diced
- 2 Italian squash, diced *(optional)*
- 3 cloves garlic, minced *(or use 2 Tbsp (17 g) garlic powder)*
- 2 Tablespoons *(14 g)* paprika
- 1 Tablespoon *(5 g)* dried oregano
- 1 Tablespoon *(9 g)* ground cumin
- 1 Tablespoon *(5 g)* dried basil
- 1 teaspoon *(2 g)* black pepper
- ¼ teaspoon *(1 g)* chili powder
- 1 teaspoon *(2 g)* cayenne pepper *(or to taste)*
- Salt to taste

INSTRUCTIONS

1. Mix everything together well in your slow cooker. Scale down the recipe if you have a smaller slow cooker.
2. Cook on low setting for 8 hours *(stir after 4 hours if you can - again the exact time may be longer depending on your slow cooker).*
3. Add salt to taste when serving.

SUBSTITUTIONS

- Pineapple chunks can be used instead of raspberries.
- Italian squash and chili peppers can be omitted.
- If you omit the ground liver, then only use 2 cans of diced tomatoes.

Slow Cooker Ropa Vieja

Prep Time: 20 minutes
Cook Time: 6 hours
Total Time: 6 hours 20 minutes
Yield: 6-8 servings
Serving Size: 1 large bowl

Ropa Vieja is an amazing Latin-American dish. If you're not familiar with it, then this recipe will blow your mind. We got one of our friends to start making this dish, and he probably ate it 3-4 times a week for the first couple months he knew about it.

INGREDIENTS

- 3 lbs *(1362 g)* flank steak
- 2 Tablespoons *(30 ml)* coconut oil *(for pan searing)*
- 1/4 cup (60 ml) olive oil
- 1 Tablespoon (15 ml) white wine vinegar *(or apple cider vinegar)*
- ¼ cup *(4 g)* cilantro, finely chopped
- ¼ cup *(15 g)* parsley, finely chopped
- 2 cloves garlic, crushed
- 2 6-ounce *(170 g)* cans tomato paste
- 3 bell peppers, sliced
- 1 Tablespoon *(7 g)* onion powder
- 1 Tablespoon *(8 g)* garlic powder
- 1 Tablespoon *(5 g)* dried oregano
- 1 Tablespoon *(10 g)* cumin powder
- Salt to taste

INSTRUCTIONS

1. Cut the flank steak into 2-inch *(5 cm)* strips. Remember to slice against the grain, as it will make the final product less chewy.

2. Place 1 Tablespoon *(14 g)* of coconut oil into a large frying pan and turn the heat to high. Pan-sear half of the flank steak strips - leave in the frying pan for around 2-3 minutes on each side. Repeat with the other half of the flank steak strips.

3. Place all ingredients plus the seared flank steak strips into the slow cooker.

4. Using your hands, make sure all the ingredients are well mixed.

5. Set slow cooker on the low heat setting and cook for 6 hours *(cooking times may vary depending on your slow cooker - the meat should shred easily)*.

Stuffed Peppers with Cinnamon Butternut Squash & Ground Beef

Prep Time: 10 minutes
Cook Time: 40 minutes
Total Time: 50 minutes
Yield: 4 servings
Serving Size: 1 stuffed pepper

You might notice that most of our recipes don't have very imaginative names. That's because we're more interested in the flavors and in the ease of cooking than we are in cool names. That's definitely true for this recipe. The title tells you exactly what you'll taste, and we promise you won't be disappointed.

INGREDIENTS

- 4 large bell peppers
- ½ lb *(227 g)* ground beef
- 2 cups *(280 g)* butternut squash, cubed
- ½ small onion, diced
- ½ cup walnuts, crushed
- 1 egg
- 2 teaspoons *(5 g)* ground cinnamon
- 2 teaspoons *(4 g)* ground cardamom
- Salt to taste
- 2 Tablespoons *(30 ml)* coconut oil to cook with
- Parsley for garnish *(optional)*

INSTRUCTIONS

1. Preheat oven to 350 F *(177 C)*.
2. Chop off the stem from each bell pepper and remove the seeds. If the pepper doesn't stand by itself, then slice off a small portion from the bottom of the pepper so that it sits flat *(but try not to create a hole in the pepper)*.
3. Sit the peppers on a baking tray and bake for 40 minutes.
4. Meanwhile, sauté the butternut squash in 1 Tablespoon *(14 g)* of coconut oil on medium heat.
5. After sautéing for 5 minutes, add the chopped onions to the butternut squash and keep sautéing.
6. In a separate pan, cook the ground beef in 1 Tablespoon *(14 g)* of coconut oil until it's browned.
7. Crack an egg into the ground beef and mix in.
8. When the onions turn translucent, add the butternut squash and onions to the ground beef and eggs.
9. Add the walnuts, cinnamon, cardamom, and salt to taste.
10. Cook until the butternut squash is tender.
11. Stuff the butternut squash/ground beef mixture into the peppers.
12. Garnish with parsley *(optional)*.

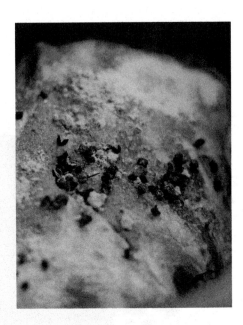

Throw-in-the-pot Slow Cooker Shredded BBQ Pork

Prep Time: 5 minutes
Cook Time: 8 hours
Total Time: 8 hours, 5 minutes
Yield: 4 servings
Serving Size: ½ lb *(227 g)*

Pork is an amazing meat. We highly encourage the purchase of humanely-raised pork if you can afford and find it, but we usually think the cheapest cuts are the best. Pork shoulder is one of those cuts, and it's the part that's often used for pulled pork.

INGREDIENTS

- 2 lbs *(908 g)* pork shoulder *(or pork shoulder collar)*
- 1 Tablespoon *(18 g)* salt *(or to taste)*
- 1 Tablespoon *(5 g)* ginger powder
- 20 Szechuan peppercorns *(omit for AIP)*
- BBQ sauce *(see page 169 for recipe) (omit for AIP)*

INSTRUCTIONS

1. Place the pork into the slow cooker *(leave the pork whole - do not cut it up)*.
2. Sprinkle all spices onto the meat.
3. Set the slow cooker for 8 hours on low heat setting.
4. Turn the pork over after 6 hours but do not pull it apart. Shred the pork when serving to prevent drying.
5. Serve with BBQ sauce *(see page 169 for recipe)* or use the meat for a pork and pineapple sauté *(see page 101 for recipe)*.

SUBSTITUTIONS

- Regular peppercorns can be used instead of Szechuan peppercorns.
- Fresh ginger slices can be used instead of ginger powder.
- For a very easy recipe, omit everything except the pork and the salt.

the **PALEO**
Essential
COOKBOOK

Pressure Cooker Garlic Turmeric "Butter" Chicken

Prep Time: 5 minutes
Cook Time: 40 minutes
Total Time: 45 minutes
Yield: 4 servings
Serving Size: 1 plate

The first time we made this dish, we were a bit skeptical about how it would turn out because it's so simple (it's got just 4 ingredients), but the garlic and the ghee made this dish both tasty and moist. We hope you give it a try.

INGREDIENTS

- 4 chicken breasts, whole or chopped
- ¼ cup turmeric ghee (or use regular ghee with 1 teaspoon turmeric powder)
- 1 teaspoon salt (add more to taste)
- 10 cloves garlic, peeled and diced

INSTRUCTIONS

1. Add the chicken breasts to the pressure cooker pot.
2. Add the ghee, salt, and diced garlic to the pressure cooker pot.
3. Set pressure cooker on high pressure for 35 minutes. Follow your pressure cooker's instructions for releasing then pressure.
4. Shred the chicken breast in the pot as soon as it's cooked.
5. Add more ghee when serving if you want.

Spaghetti Squash Bolognese

Prep Time: 10 minutes
Cook Time: 50 minutes
Total Time: 1 hour
Yield: 4 servings
Serving Size: 1 large bowl

There are a variety of ways to make pasta without the wheat. The most popular way (and still our favorite) is to use spaghetti squash. If you don't have this handy, then zucchinis works well too - you'll need a julienne peeler to create the strands.

INGREDIENTS

- 1 spaghetti squash
- 2 lb *(900 g)* ground or minced beef
- 1 onion, diced
- 1.5 6 oz (170 g) cans of tomato paste
- 1.5 14.5 oz (410 g) cans of diced tomato
- 1 cup *(40 g)* fresh basil, finely chopped
- 8 cloves garlic, crushed
- Coconut oil to cook with
- Salt and pepper to taste

INSTRUCTIONS

1. Cook the onions in a large pot with coconut oil. Add the ground beef.
3. Once the meat is browned, add the tomato paste and diced tomatoes and simmer with the lid on for 30 minutes (simmer for 1 hour if you have time). Stir regularly to make sure it's not sticking to the bottom of the pot.
4. Meanwhile, chop a spaghetti squash in half, remove the seeds (you can roast the seeds for a snack), cover the insides with a thin layer of coconut oil (you can use your hands to do this), cover with a paper towel to avoid splattering, and microwave each half for 6-7 minutes on high.
5. Use a fork to scratch out the spaghetti squash strands and divide between 4 plates.
6. Add the basil, garlic, salt, and pepper to taste to the meat sauce, cook for 5 more minutes, and top onto the spaghetti squash.

SUBSTITUTIONS

- Other ground or minced meat may be substituted for the beef.
- Italian seasoning can be used instead of basil and garlic powder instead of fresh garlic. Both and the onion can be omitted.

Chapter 4:
Side Dishes

Apple Pecan Brussels Sprouts

Prep Time: 10 minutes
Cook Time: 20 minutes
Total Time: 30 minutes
Yield: 2 servings
Serving Size: a large bowl

Bacon makes everything better, but when it comes to Brussels sprouts (one of our favorite veggies), bacon is an almost magical addition. And it's even better when you cook the Brussels sprouts in the bacon fat. Try it and love it.

INGREDIENTS

- 1 lb *(454 g)* Brussels sprouts, finely chopped
- 1 medium apple, peeled and diced
- 2-3 slices of bacon, uncooked, chopped into small pieces
- ½ cup *(50 g)* pecans, chopped *(omit for AIP)*
- Salt to taste

INSTRUCTIONS

1. Toss the bacon pieces into a large frying pan and let it cook until almost crispy.
3. Add in the Brussels sprouts and sauté.
4. After 5 minutes, add in the apple pieces, and sauté for a few more minutes.
5. Last, add in the pecans, and sauté until the Brussels sprouts are as soft as you prefer.
6. Add salt to taste.

SUBSTITUTIONS

- Pancetta pieces can be used instead of bacon.
- A pear can be used instead of an apple.

Carrot and Apple Hash
with Cinnamon and Ginger

Prep Time: 10 minutes
Cook Time: 10 minutes
Total Time: 20 minutes
Yield: 2 servings
Serving Size: 1 small plate

When you taste this dish, you'll understand why it doesn't need any additional ingredients. The apple and carrots soften, and their natural sugars ooze out to mingle with the coconut oil making you savor every single bite of this dish. Perfect as a tasty side dish, a snack, or for breakfast!

INGREDIENTS

- 1 medium carrot, shredded
- 1 apple, peeled and shredded
- 3 Tablespoons *(45 ml)* coconut oil for cooking
- Cinnamon *(for sprinkling)*
- Fresh ginger *(for topping)*

INSTRUCTIONS

1. Squeeze out any excess water from the carrots and apples.
2. Mix the apples and carrots together and pour 3 Tablespoons *(41 g)* of coconut oil into the skillet/frying-pan.
3. Form 2 large flat patties in the skillet/frying-pan and fry on medium heat
(2-3 minutes on each side – be careful when turning and check it doesn't burn). Use a spatula to press down on the patties to help them cook better.
4. Serve with a sprinkling of cinnamon and freshly grated ginger.

Cauliflower White "Rice"

Prep Time: 10 minutes
Cook Time: 15 minutes
Total Time: 25 minutes
Yield: 2 servings
Serving Size: 1 cup

When we first made rice out of cauliflower (after seeing it on Michelle Tam's site), we were incredibly surprised by how much it resembled the rice we were used to. And when we made it for our friends, they were even more surprised. This is the most basic of the cauliflower rice recipes - you can add your favorite meats and veggies to this recipe if you want.

INGREDIENTS
- ½ head *(approx. 220 g)* of cauliflower
- 1 Tablespoon *(15 ml)* coconut oil
- Salt to taste

INSTRUCTIONS
1. Cut up the cauliflower into small florets so that they'll fit into a food processor.
2. Process the cauliflower in the food processor until it forms very small "rice"-like pieces. Squeeze out excess water.
3. Add 1 Tablespoon of coconut oil into a large pot. Add in the cauliflower and let it cook on a medium heat. Stir regularly to make sure it doesn't burn!
4. Cook until tender but not mushy. Add salt and serve.

Garlic Lemon Broccolini Saute

Prep Time: 5 minutes
Cook Time: 10 minutes
Total Time: 15 minutes
Yield: 2 servings
Serving Size: 1 plate

Louise loves a good vegetable side dish to her meals, and this one is simple and tasty. It's especially good as a side dish to steaks.

INGREDIENTS

- ½ lb *(250 g)* broccolini
- 3 cloves garlic, minced
- 1 Tablespoon *(15 ml)* lemon juice
- 1 Tablespoon *(8 g)* garlic powder (optional)
- 2 Tablespoons *(30 ml)* olive oil
- Salt to taste

INSTRUCTIONS

1. Add the olive oil into the saute pan on medium heat.
2. Add in the broccolini and saute for 5 minutes (parboil the broccolini first if you prefer it softer).
3. Add in the minced garlic, lemon juice, garlic powder, and salt.
4. Saute for a few more minutes and serve immediately.

SUBSTITUTIONS

- Chopped broccoli can be used instead of broccolini.

Creamy Mashed Sweet Potatoes

Prep Time: 15 minutes
Cooking Time: 30 minutes
Total Time: 45 minutes
Yield: 4 servings
Serving Size: 1 cup *(approx.)*

Sometimes, it's the simplest dishes that you make over and over again, but also which really impress guests. This is one of those recipes. We often make it as a side when we have friends over for dinner, and it's always the dish that empties most quickly.

INGREDIENTS

- 4 sweet potatoes
- 1 cup *(240 ml)* coconut cream *(or coconut milk)*
- 1 teaspoon *(2 g)* freshly grated ginger
- 2 Tablespoons *(9 g)* shredded coconut for topping

INSTRUCTIONS

1. Bake the sweet potatoes at 350 F *(177 C)* for about an hour. Or alternatively, boil the sweet potatoes for about 30 minutes. In either case, make sure the sweet potatoes are very tender - you should be able to poke a fork into them with ease. *(You can also microwave or steam the sweet potatoes to soften them.)*
2. Let the sweet potatoes cool for a bit and then peel them.
3. Place the peeled sweet potatoes into a food processor with the coconut milk and ginger, and food process on high until smooth.
4. Place the mashed sweet potatoes into a large bowl and top with shredded coconut.

SUBSTITUTIONS

- Potatoes, cauliflower, butternut squash, pumpkin, or squash can be used instead of sweet potatoes for a different flavor.

Easy Bacon Brussels Sprouts

Prep Time: 5 minutes
Cook Time: 20 minutes
Total Time: 25 minutes
Yield: 4-6 servings
Serving Size: 1 cup *(approx.)*

If we're being completely honest, we worried a lot about putting some of our simplest recipes in this book. We sometimes feel like these recipes aren't "special" enough or unique enough. But when it comes down to it, these are the recipes that we personally make all the time. And we know that for you to be successful in the long-run, it's about having recipes you can prepare quickly (and over and over again), rather than a lot of complicated recipes.

INGREDIENTS

- 2 lbs *(908 g)* Brussels sprouts
- 1 lb *(454 g)* bacon, uncooked

INSTRUCTIONS

1. Boil the Brussels sprouts for 10 minutes until tender.
2. While the Brussels sprouts are boiling, chop the bacon into small pieces *(approx. ½-inch wide)*, and cook the bacon pieces in a large pot on medium heat. When the bacon is crispy, add in the drained Brussels sprouts.
4. Cook for 10 more minutes, mixing occasionally to make sure nothing gets burnt on the bottom of the pan.

Fried Sweet Plantains

Prep Time: 10 minutes
Cook Time: 30 minutes
Total Time: 40 minutes
Yield: 2 servings
Serving Size: approx.15 pieces

When we were living in Astoria, New York, we used to eat out at the Brazilian Churrascarias around our neighborhood. A Churrascaria is essentially a Brazilian restaurant that barbecues a lot of different meat. But in addition to the meat (fish, veggies, and salads), they often also had fried sweet plantains, which we both absolutely love. *(The ones at the restaurants have added sugar and bad oils, but ours are perfect.)*

INGREDIENTS
- 2 ripe plantains
- 4 Tablespoons *(60 ml)* coconut oil for frying

INSTRUCTIONS
1. Peel the plantains and cut into 3 chunks lengthwise. Thinly slice each chunk to form long 4-5 thin strips *(not round slices)*.
2. Place 4 Tablespoons *(55 g)* of coconut oil into pan on low heat.
3. Place the plantains strips into the pan and cook gently.
4. Flip the plantain strips after 10-15 minutes and cook the other side.
5. Keep cooking and turning for 30-40 minutes until the plantains are soft.

SUBSTITUTIONS
- Bananas can be used instead of plantains.

Green Beans and Apples

Prep Time: 5 minutes
Cook Time: 20 minutes
Total Time: 25 minutes
Yield: 2 servings
Serving Size: 1 cup

We are super-proud of this recipe. Green beans and apples isn't a combination that is very common, much less with curry powder. But we've made this probably 30-40 times, because it's just so good *(and so easy)*. Give it a try and let us know what you think.

INGREDIENTS

- 12 ounces *(340 g)* green beans *(fresh or frozen)*
- 1 green apple, cored and sliced thinly
- 1 clove garlic, minced
- ½ teaspoon *(1 g)* curry powder
- Salt to taste
- 1 Tablespoon *(15 ml)* coconut oil to cook in

INSTRUCTIONS

1. Boil the green beans until tender *(you can parboil them if you prefer crisper beans)*.
2. Drain the boiled green beans.
3. Add 1 tablespoon of coconut oil into a skillet *(or saucepan)*. Add into the skillet the green beans and apple slices. Sauté until the apples are tender *(5-10 minutes)*.
4. Stir in the minced garlic, curry powder, and salt.

SUBSTITUTIONS

- Garam masala can be used instead of curry powder.

Mushrooms with Red Wine and Rosemary

Prep Time: 5 minutes
Cook Time: 15 minutes
Total Time: 20 minutes
Yield: 2 servings
Serving Size: ¼ cup

Mushrooms are under-used in most Paleo cookbooks *(in our opinion)*, so we wanted to be sure to include one good recipe featuring mushrooms. It really helps to have very fresh rosemary, as it makes a huge difference for the flavor.

INGREDIENTS

- 1 sprig of rosemary
- 10-12 medium-sized button mushrooms *(approx. ½ lb (227 g))*, sliced
- 2 Tablespoons *(30 ml)* ghee *(or coconut oil) (for AIP use coconut oil)*
- ¼ cup *(60 ml)* red wine *(omit for AIP)*
- Salt to taste

INSTRUCTIONS

1. Place the ghee or coconut oil into a frying pan.
2. Add the rosemary and then the sliced mushrooms.
3. Sauté the mushrooms on medium heat until they've soaked in most of the ghee and are soft *(approx. 5-7 minutes)*.
4. Pour in the red wine and add in salt and pepper.
5. Keep cooking until pretty much no liquid is left in the pan.

SUBSTITUTIONS

- Red wine can be omitted.

Parsnip Fries

Prep Time: 10 minutes
Cook Time: 40 minutes
Total Time: 50 minutes
Yield: 4 servings
Serving Size: 1 bowl

We noted in another recipes that Jeremy has fallen in love with parsnips recently. A lot of people make sweet potato fries, and those are certainly delicious, but we encourage you to branch out and try these parsnip fries, which actually add a lot of flavor. We love topping chili on them to create a complete meal *(see page 65 for recipe)*. Thanks to Alison Golden from PaleoNonPaleo.com for introducing parsnip fries to us!

INGREDIENTS

- 4 parsnips, peeled and cut into fries
- ¼ cup *(15 g)* parsley, finely chopped
- ¼ cup *(60 ml)* olive oil
- 1 Tablespoon *(18 g)* salt
- 1 teaspoon *(2 g)* pepper *(omit for AIP)*

INSTRUCTIONS

1. Preheat oven to 450 F *(232 C)*.
2. Toss all the ingredients together in a large bowl and spread the fries onto a baking tray.
3. Bake for 40 minutes.

SUBSTITUTIONS

- Parsley can be omitted.
- Sweet potatoes can be used instead of parsnips.

Roasted Turmeric Cauliflower

Prep Time: 15 minutes
Cook Time: 1 hour, 15 minutes
Total Time: 1 hour, 30 minutes
Servings: 4 servings
Yield: 1 small bowl

Someone at a dinner party once told us that turmeric went amazing well with cauliflower. Louise was highly skeptical, but she just had to try it out. They were completely correct - turmeric and cauliflower go superbly together. So, if you're also skeptical, then we urge to give this simple recipe a try before passing judgment.

INGREDIENTS

- Half of a large cauliflower
- 2 teaspoons *(5 g)* turmeric
- 2 teaspoons *(12 g)* salt
- 2 Tablespoons *(30 ml)* olive oil

INSTRUCTIONS

1. Preheat oven to 350 F *(177 C)*.
2. Separate the cauliflower florets from the cauliflower stem. Discard the stem.
3. Combine the cauliflower florets with the turmeric, salt, and olive oil.
4. Place in baking dish *(spread out the cauliflower so they're not on top of each other)*.
5. Cover the baking dish with foil.
6. Bake for 75 minutes.

Rosemary Roasted Vegetables

Prep Time: 15 minutes
Cook Time: 50 minutes
Total Time: 1 hour 5 minutes
Yield: 6-8 servings
Serving Size: 1 cup *(approx.)*

We can't recommend this recipe highly enough. It's one of 4-5 recipes that we eat all the time. It takes a little while to cook, but the vegetables come out so deliciously. It's also really easy to double this recipe and make an extra large batch if you have a big oven.

INGREDIENTS

- 3 sweet potatoes, diced *(4-5 cups (532-665 g))*
- ½ butternut squash, diced *(2-3 cups (280-420 g))*
- 2 red bell peppers, chopped *(omit for AIP)*
- 1 leek, chopped *(or use 1 onion)*
- ½ cup *(120 ml)* olive oil
- ¼ cup *(7 g)* fresh rosemary, chopped
- 2 Tablespoons *(5 g)* fresh thyme, chopped
- ½ Tablespoon *(9g)* salt, or to taste

INSTRUCTIONS

1. Preheat oven to 400 F *(204 C)*.
2. Mix the olive oil, rosemary, thyme, and salt together in a large bowl.
3. Place the diced sweet potatoes and butternut squash into the olive oil bowl and mix well.
4. Line a large baking tray with foil. Remove the sweet potatoes and butternut squash from the bowl and spread onto the baking tray. Place in oven for 20 minutes.
5. Meanwhile, place the leek and peppers into the bowl with the remaining olive oil mixture and mix well.
6. After the sweet potatoes/butternut squash have cooked for 20 minutes, add the leeks and peppers (and any remaining olive oil mixture) onto the baking tray, and with a spatula or wooden spoon, carefully mix the vegetables together. *(Adding the leeks and peppers too early may cause them to burn.)*
7. Bake for 20-30 more minutes until everything is tender.

SUBSTITUTIONS

• An onion, chopped, can be used instead of the leek.
• Potatoes, pumpkin, or squash can be used instead of the sweet potatoes for a different taste.

Sesame Cucumber Mash

Prep Time: 15 minutes
Cooking Time: 0 minutes
Total Time: 15 minutes
Yield: 1 serving
Serving Size: 1 cup

One of our favorite recipes during the summer is the
simple cucumber salad (chilled cucumber chunks with freshly minced garlic, olive oil,
and salt). But for some more variation during the summer months, we started making this easy
cucumber mash instead. It's refreshing and won't weigh you down at all!

INGREDIENTS

- 1 cucumber *(12 oz or 340 g)* - peeled and cut into large chunks to fit into blender
- 5 small basil leaves (or 3 large leaves)
- Juice from ¼ lime
- ¼ cup *(60 ml)* water to get blender going
- 1 teaspoon *(5 ml)* sesame oil *(use olive oil for AIP)*
- 1 teaspoon *(3 g)* garlic powder or to taste
- Salt to taste

INSTRUCTIONS

1. Place the cucumber, basil, lime juice, and water into a blender and blend well.
2. Using a strainer, squeeze the liquid out of the cucumber mash.
3. Mix in the sesame oil, garlic powder, and salt.
4. Enjoy chilled!

Super Fast Avocado Salad

Prep Time: 5 minutes
Cooking Time: 0 minutes
Total Time: 5 minutes
Yield: 1 serving
Serving Size: 1 cup

There is nothing tricky about this recipe. The first time we made it, we asked ourselves why we hadn't done it before. Doesn't matter. Just try it. It's also great as a fast and very filling breakfast!

INGREDIENTS

- 1 ripe avocado
- 1 Tablespoon *(15 ml)* olive oil
- 1 Tablespoon *(15 ml)* balsamic vinegar
- Salt to taste

INSTRUCTIONS

1. Cut a ripe avocado in half.
2. Remove the pit, and using a small knife carefully score each half into cubes. Then use a spoon to scoop out the avocado - it'll be in nice cubes now.
3. Toss the avocado cubes with olive oil, balsamic vinegar, and salt.

Sweet Potato Tater Tots

Prep Time: 15 minutes
Cook Time: 30 minutes
Total Time: 45 minutes
Yield: 4 servings
Serving Size: 10-15 tater tots

Tater tots weren't part of Louise's childhood, but they were part of Jeremy's, which is why we decided to create a healthier version of them without the wheat flour and without the canola oil!

INGREDIENTS

- 2 large sweet potatoes, peeled and cubed *(approx. 4 cups (532 g))*
- 4 Tablespoons *(28 g)* coconut flour
- ½ teaspoon *(3 g)* salt

INSTRUCTIONS

1. Preheating the oven to 425 F *(218 C)*.
2. Steam the sweet potato cubes until just soft *(approx. 15 minutes – you don't want them too soft)*. Alternatively, bake or microwave the sweet potatoes.
3. In a food processor or blender, mix together the sweet potatoes (make sure they're not too hot and pour out any water from the steamer), coconut flour, and salt.
4. Form the mixture into small balls *(with your hands or a mini ice-cream scoop or a spoon)*.
5. Place the balls onto a parchment paper lined baking sheet and bake for 15 minutes.

SUBSTITUTIONS

- Potatoes or pumpkin can be used instead of the sweet potatoes for a different taste.

the **PALEO**
COOKBOOK

Pressure Cooker Beet Cabbage Apple Stew

Prep Time: 10 minutes
Cook Time: 30 minutes
Total Time: 40 minutes
Yield: 4 servings

Serving Size: 1 bowl

We love how easy this recipe is. If you're looking to get more veggies into your Paleo diet, then this recipe is a quick and delicious way to do so. Just toss everything into the pressure cooker, and enjoy!

INGREDIENTS

- 4 cups *(1 l)* chicken broth or bone broth
- 1 apple *(200 g)*, diced
- 1/2 head of cabbage *(454 g)*, chopped
- 1 small onion *(140 g)*, chopped
- 2 beets *(200 g)*, chopped
- 2 small carrots *(115 g)*, chopped
- 1 Tablespoon fresh ginger *(6 g)*, grated
- 1 teaspoon *(2 g)* gelatin (optional)
- 2 Tablespoons *(4 g)* parsley
- Salt to taste

INSTRUCTIONS

1. Place everything into the pressure cooker. Cook on high pressure for 20 minutes. When ready, follow your pressure cooker's instructions for releasing the pressure safely.

SUBSTITUTIONS

• Change up the vegetables to suit what's available at your local grocery store.

Chapter 5:
Desserts

Breads

Amazing Chocolate Chip Muffins

Prep Time: 10 minutes
Cook Time: 20 minutes
Total Time: 30 minutes
Yield: 12 muffins
Serving Size: 2 muffins

To be honest, we don't eat very many desserts. That probably makes us a little bit weird, but we'd usually rather just eat more non-dessert foods. That said, we've definitely made these muffins more than a few times. *(But we try not to do it too often, because we usually end up eating the entire batch in a day or so.)*

INGREDIENTS

- 3 cups *(285 g)* almond flour
- 1 teaspoon *(4 g)* baking soda
- ½ cup *(120 ml)* ghee, melted
- 4 eggs, whisked
- 1 Tablespoon *(21 g)* raw honey
- 1 cup *(150 g)* chocolate chips
- 1 Tablespoon *(15 ml)* vanilla extract

INSTRUCTIONS

1. Preheat oven to 350 F *(175 C)*.
2. Mix all the ingredients together (you don't need a whisk) except for the chocolate chips.
3. Add in the chocolate chips to the mixture last and gently mix in.
4. Pour mixture into muffin pan *(makes 12 muffins)*.
5. Bake in oven for 18-20 minutes.

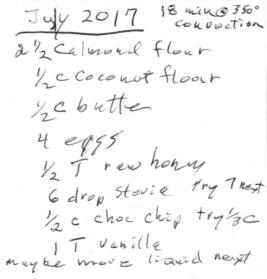

July 2017   18 min @ 350°
convection
2½ C almond flour
½ c coconut flour
½ c butter
4 eggs
½ T raw honey
6 drop stevia try 7 next
½ c choc chip try ¼ c
1 T vanilla
maybe more liquid next

the **Essential PALEO** COOKBOOK

Cinnamon Sugar Pretzel Bites

Prep Time: 15 minutes
Cook Time: 15 minutes
Total Time: 30 minutes
Yield: 4 servings
Serving Size: 10 pretzel bites *(approx.)*

You probably know this, but some recipes take many tries to get right. This is one of those recipes. We had to make it probably 10 times before we were satisfied with it, but once we did, we were very pleased. *(Your kids will love this one.)*

INGREDIENTS

For the pretzel bites
- 3 eggs
- 1½ cups *(143 g)* almond flour
- 2 Tablespoons *(26 g)* ghee, melted
- 3 Tablespoons *(21 g)* coconut flour
- 1 teaspoon *(7 g)* raw honey

For the coating
- 1/4 cup *(36 g)* coconut sugar
- 1 Tablespoon *(8 g)* ground cinnamon
- 1/4 cup *(60 ml)* ghee, melted

INSTRUCTIONS

1. Preheat oven to 350 F *(177 C)*.
2. Place all the pretzel bites ingredients (eggs, almond flour, ghee, coconut flour, and honey) into a bowl and mix well (with your hands) until it forms a dough.
3. Let the dough sit for 5 minutes.
4. Roll into pretzel bites *(small balls)* and place on a parchment paper lined baking tray.
5. Bake in oven for 6-7 minutes.
6. Take the pretzels out and heat oven to 400 F *(204 C)*.
7. Turn each pretzel bite over, place back in oven, and bake for 4-5 more minutes.
8. Meanwhile, in another bowl, combine the cinnamon and the coconut sugar.
9. Remove pretzel bites from oven, let cool, and dip each into the melted ghee and then into the cinnamon and coconut sugar mix.
10. For a less sweet option, brush the top of each pretzel bite with ghee and sprinkle the cinnamon and coconut sugar mix over them.

SUBSTITUTIONS

- Coconut sugar can be used instead of honey in the pretzel bites dough mixture.

Double Chocolate Coconut Ice Cream

Prep Time: 4 hours
Cook Time: 0 minutes
Total Time: 4 hours
Yield: 2 servings
Serving Size: 1 cup

If you're going to make ice cream *(and who doesn't love ice cream)*, then we highly recommend getting an ice cream maker. If you don't have one, then it requires a lot more attention, and even with the extra attention, it's tough to keep the ice cream from getting too icy. We've run into this problem on many, many occasions.

INGREDIENTS

- 1 cup *(240 ml)* coconut cream *(or, alternatively use the top layer of cream from a refrigerated can of coconut milk)*
- 1 Tablespoon *(21 g)* raw honey
- ½ cup *(60 g)* cacao powder
- ¼ cup *(25 g)* chocolate chips *(optional)*
- 1 teaspoon *(5 ml)* sugar-free, gluten-free vanilla extract
- Dash of salt

INSTRUCTIONS

1. Whisk all the ingredients *(except the chocolate chips)* together well - you might need to melt the coconut cream and honey slightly depending on how cold your kitchen is.

2. Add in the chocolate chips last *(making sure the mixture isn't too warm when you add them)*.

3. Place the mixture into your ice cream maker and follow its instructions for making ice cream.

4. If you're not using an ice cream maker, then pour the mixture into a large bowl and place into the freezer. Stir the mixture every 30 minutes for 3-4 hours until it forms an ice cream consistency.

Cardamom Orange Walnut Truffles

Prep Time: 5 minutes
Wait Time: 2 hours
Total Time: 2 hours and 5 minutes
Yield: 4-6 servings
Serving Size: 2-3 pieces

These truffles are delicious anytime, and if you make them with stevia, then they can be a great low-carb dessert as well. The orange and cardamom mix is really good!

INGREDIENTS

- 1 cup almond butter (or walnut butter)
- ¼ cup coconut oil
- 2 teaspoons orange zest
- 1/3 cup walnuts
- ¼ cup unsweetened coconut flakes (or shredded coconut)
- Dash of cardamom
- 1 Tablespoon cacao powder (optional)
- Stevia to taste (or use raw honey to taste)
- 1/2 cup unsweetened shredded coconut

INSTRUCTIONS

1. Place all the ingredients except for the shredded coconut into a blender and blend well. Taste the mixture and add more stevia or raw honey to taste.
2. Place in fridge or freezer to solidify a bit.
3. Form small balls from the mixture.
4. Roll the balls in the remaining ¼ cup shredded coconut.
5. Place in fridge to set.

Double-layered Chocolate Cake
with Chocolate Frosting and Ganache

Prep Time: 60 minutes
Cook Time: 30 minutes
Total Time: 1 hour 30 minutes
Yield: one 9-inch cake *(2 layers)*
Serving Size: one slice, *(approx. 1/8 of cake)*

We only make cakes for special occasions, and we made this one for a birthday. We didn't really know what to expect, but this is a recipe that turned out quite brilliantly on the first try. Perhaps that's because it's got so much chocolate in it, and if there's one thing that Louise loves, it's chocolate.

INGREDIENTS

For the cakes:
- 3 cups *(285 g)* almond flour
- 1/3 cup *(28 g)* pure whey protein powder
- 1½ teaspoons *(7 g)* baking powder
- ½ cup *(43 g)* cocoa powder
- 1 teaspoon *(5 g)* baking soda
- Pinch of salt
- 1 cup *(240 ml)* coconut oil, softened *(or use ghee)*
- 3 large eggs
- 1 Tablespoon *(15 ml)* vanilla extract
- 4 Tablespoons *(84 g)* raw honey
- ¾ cup *(177 ml)* almond milk

For the Chocolate Coconut Ganache:
- ½ cup *(120 ml)* coconut milk
- ½ cup *(66 g)* chocolate chips, melted
- 1 teaspoon (5 ml) vanilla extract
- 3 Tablespoons *(14 g)* shredded coconut *(optional)*

For the Chocolate Frosting:
- 1 cup *(132 g)* chocolate chips, melted
- 1/3 cup *(78 ml)* coconut oil, melted
- 1 teaspoon *(5 ml)* vanilla extract

INSTRUCTIONS

1. Preheat oven to 300 F (149 C).
2. Mix together all ingredients for the cake in a large bowl.
3. Line two 9-inch cake pans with parchment paper *(base and sides)*.
4. Divide the cake batter between the 2 pans and bake for 30 minutes *(check the cake is done by inserting a cocktail stick or toothpick and making sure it comes out clean)*.
5. While the cake is baking, mix together the ingredients for the chocolate coconut ganache and place in fridge to thicken.
6. Mix together the ingredients for the chocolate frosting and refrigerate for approx. 15 minutes *(it's ok if you refrigerate it for longer)*.
7. When the cakes are done, let them cool for at least 30 minutes *(otherwise the ganache and frosting will melt on the cake!)*.
8. If the tops of the cakes are not flat, then you can gently cut off the top of one of them to make it flatter.
9. Spread ganache on one of the cakes and place the other cake on top of the first cake to form the top layer.
10. Stir the chocolate frosting gently with a fork to make it form a frosting consistency *(if it's too hard, then let it melt a bit at room temperature, or if it's too "liquid-y", place it back in the fridge for a bit)*.
11. Spread the frosting on the cake and add any additional decorations you want.

Make-All-The-Time
Chocolate Chip Cookies

Prep Time: 15 minutes
Cook Time: 12 minutes
Total Time: 27 minutes
Yield: 5-6 servings
Serving Size: 3-4 cookies

Despite the name, we don't actually recommend making these cookies "all the time," even if you find yourself wanting to. They're too yummy, and it's hard to stop eating them. So while the ingredients are all Paleo and nutritious, they're very easy to overeat. Do make them instead of regular cookies though!

INGREDIENTS

- 1½ cups *(143 g)* almond flour
- ½ cup *(56 g)* coconut flour
- ¼ cup *(43 g)* shredded coconut
- 2 teaspoons *(10 ml)* vanilla extract
- 2-3 Tablespoons *(42-63 g)* raw honey
- 2 eggs, whisked
- ½ cup *(120 ml)* ghee, melted
- ½ cup *(66 g)* chocolate chips
- Dash of salt

INSTRUCTIONS

1. Preheat oven to 325 F (163 C) and place parchment paper on a baking tray.
2. Mix all ingredients together in a large mixing bowl (add the chocolate chips in after everything else has been mixed together well).
3. Form small 2-inch diameter cookies and place on baking tray. It should make around 20 cookies.
4. Bake for 12 minutes. Remove baking tray from oven and cool for a few minutes before removing cookies from baking tray.

Tasty Apple Tartlets

Prep Time: 15 minutes
Cook Time: 40 minutes
Total Time: 55 minutes
Yield: 6 servings
Serving Size: 2 tartlets

You can make these any time of year, but in the US, this type of dessert is most popular around the fall and winter holidays. We guarantee that if you make these and take them to the office or to a party, nobody will complain about them being Paleo *(they likely won't even notice)*.

INGREDIENTS

Crust
- 2 cups *(240 g)* almond flour
- ¾ cup *(84 g)* coconut flour
- 4 eggs, whisked
- 3 Tablespoons *(45 ml)* ghee (or coconut oil), melted
- 4 Tablespoons *(19 g)* shredded coconut
- 2 Tablespoons *(30 ml)* vanilla extract

Filling
- 6 apples, peeled, cored and thinly sliced
- 1 Tablespoon *(21 g)* raw honey *(optional)*
- 3 Tablespoons *(45 ml)* coconut oil
- 2-3 Tablespoons *(15-30 ml)* vanilla extract
- 1 teaspoon *(2 g)* ground cardamom
- 1 teaspoon *(3 g)* ground cinnamon
- Freshly grated lemon zest for garnish

INSTRUCTIONS

1. Preheat oven to 350 F (175 C).
2. Mix together all the crust ingredients in a mixing bowl using your hands until it becomes dough-like. Don't worry that the dough won't stretch or feels a bit crumbly.
3. Get a small amount of the dough and place into each space in the muffin pan. Using your hands, spread the dough so that it forms a crust (it'll be a bit thicker than traditional tart crusts).
4. Bake in the oven for 15 minutes and leave to cool when it's done.
5. Meanwhile, melt the coconut oil in a saucepan and add in all the other filling ingredients *(apple slices, optional honey, vanilla extract, and spices)*.
6. Let the apple slices cook for 20-30 minutes until it's very soft.
7. Pour the apple filling into a bowl to cool for 10 minutes.
8. Spoon the apple filling into each tartlet crust so that it's level with the top of the crust. Then take 5-6 individual slices of apple for each tartlet and layer them in a cascade on the top covering the filling. Place the last slice facing the other way *(see photo)*.
9. Grate some fresh lemon zest on top for garnish.

Garlic Cauliflower Naan Bread

Prep Time: 10 minutes
Cook Time: 15 minutes
Total Time: 25 minutes
Yield: 1 serving
Serving Size: 1 naan bread

One of our most popular recipes is the microwave bread recipe, but for this edition of the cookbook, we decided to switch things up and include this amazing new bread recipe Louise came up with instead.

Enjoy this naan bread with the coconut chicken curry dish!

INGREDIENTS

- ½ cup *(64g)* arrowroot flour
- 1 cup *(5 oz or 140 g)* cauliflower florets
- 1 Tablespoon *(8 g)* garlic powder
- 2 Tablespoons *(30 ml)* avocado oil
- Salt to taste

INSTRUCTIONS

1. Preheat oven to 450 F (230 C).
2. Place the cauliflower florets into a bowl with some water and microwave on high until tender (check every 2 minutes to make sure it doesn't burn). Alternatively, steam the florets until tender.
3. Food process (or use a blender) to process the cauliflower florets into a mash.
4. Mix the cauliflower mash with the arrowroot flour, garlic powder, avocado oil, and salt. Taste the mixture and add in more garlic powder and salt to taste. Mix into a springy dough.
5. Use your hands to press the dough into a flat bread, place on some parchment paper, and bake in oven for 15 minutes.
6. Let cool and serve.

the
Essential **PALEO**
COOKBOOK

Freshly Baked Loaf of Bread

Prep Time: 10 minutes
Cook Time: 1 hour
Total Time: 1 hour, 10 minutes
Yield: 1 loaf of bread
Serving Size: 2 slices

Since we've been Paleo for quite a while, we don't make Paleo breads very often. But sometimes we just really want it *(Louise in particular)*. This is our absolute best bread recipe. It's not nearly as quick as the microwave bread, but it turns out fluffy and just like "normal" bread.

INGREDIENTS

- 3 cups *(330g)* almond flour
- ½ cup + 2 Tablespoons *(150 ml)* olive oil *(or coconut oil)*
- ¼ cup (60 ml) almond milk *(or water)*
- 3 eggs
- 2 teaspoons *(9 g)* baking powder
- 1 teaspoon *(5 g)* baking soda
- ¼ teaspoon *(2 g)* salt

INSTRUCTIONS

1. Preheat oven to 300 F *(149 C)*.
2. Grease a loaf pan *(9 in by 5 in (22.5 cm by 12.5 cm))* with olive oil or coconut oil.
3. Mix together all ingredients in a large bowl.
4. Pour the batter into the pan and spread it out so that it fills the pan evenly.
5. Bake for 60 minutes.
6. Let cool, flip pan, and cut into slices with a bread knife.

Jalapeño Corn Bread

Prep Time: 10 minutes
Cook Time: 20 minutes
Total Time: 30 minutes
Yield: 12 muffins
Serving Size: 2 muffins

One time, before we were Paleo, we were in Georgia visiting Jeremy's mom. We decided to make cornbread that day, and we made a "Mexican" version that we found in a recipe online. It was the best cornbread we'd ever had. So if you're wondering why we included a Paleo Jalapeño Corn Bread Recipe in this cookbook, now you know.

INGREDIENTS

- ¾ cup *(90 g)* almond flour
- ¼ cup *(30 g)* coconut flour
- 2 teaspoons *(9 g)* baking powder
- 1 teaspoon *(6 g)* salt
- 2 Tablespoons *(42 g)* raw honey
- 3 eggs
- ½ cup *(120 ml)* coconut milk
- 3 jalapeño peppers, diced

INSTRUCTIONS

1. Preheat oven to 350 F *(177 C)*.
2. Grease muffin pan with coconut oil or use muffin liners or a silicone muffin pan.
3. Mix together all ingredients well in a large bowl.
4. Pour the batter into the muffin pan.
5. Bake for 20 minutes.

SUBSTITUTIONS

- Almond milk can be used instead of coconut milk.
- Another Paleo sugar can be used instead of raw honey.

Chapter 6: Condiments, Sauces, and Dressings

Snacks

Luxuriously Simple Bone Broth

Prep Time: 5 minutes
Cook Time: 10 hours
Total Time: 10 hours 5 minutes
Yield: 8-16 servings *(depends on size of crockpot)*
Serving Size: 1 cup *(approx.)*

This recipe is so simple that you really don't need a recipe. But we couldn't leave it out, because it's the base of almost all of our soups and stews. In fact, in our house, we usually have one slow cooker on low 24 hours per day with bones and broth in it. There's nothing we make and use more.

INGREDIENTS

- 3-4 lbs *(1361-1814 g)* of bones *(I typically use beef bones)*
- 1 gallon *(3.8 l)* water *(adjust for your slow cooker size)*
- 2 Tablespoons *(30 ml)* apple cider vinegar

INSTRUCTIONS

1. Add everything to the slow cooker.
2. Cook on the low setting in slow cooker for 10 hours.
3. Cool the broth, then strain and pour broth into a container.
4. Store the broth in the refrigerator until you're ready to use.
5. Scoop out the congealed fat on top of the broth *(optional, but the broth is otherwise very fatty)*.
6. Heat broth when needed *(with spices, vegetables, etc)*.

SUGGESTIONS

• After you've made the first batch of broth, you can make additional batches with the same bones. Typically, bones will last for at least 4-5 batches of broth.

SUBSTITUTIONS

• Lemon or lime juice *(or anything else acidic)* can be used instead of apple cider vinegar - you can also omit it (it's often suggested to help draw more minerals out of the bones).

BBQ Sauce

Prep Time: 10 minutes
Cook Time: 0 minutes
Total Time: 10 minutes
Yield: approx. ¾ cup
Serving: approx. 1/8 cup

Jeremy grew up in Georgia, where grilling and barbecuing is a way of life. This is our favorite BBQ sauce *(after much testing)* - it goes great with a lot of dishes!

INGREDIENTS

- 1 6 oz *(170 g)* can of tomato paste
- ½ cup *(120 ml)* of water
- 3 Tablespoons *(45 ml)* apple cider vinegar
- 1 Tablespoon *(8 g)* garlic powder
- 1 Tablespoon *(7 g)* onion powder
- 1 teaspoon *(2.5 g)* gelatin powder
- 1 teaspoon *(2.5 g)* cinnamon
- ½ teaspoon *(1 g)* nutmeg
- ½ teaspoon *(4 g)* raw honey
- ¼ teaspoon *(0.5 g)* cloves
- 1 Tablespoon *(15 ml)* tamari soy sauce
- 1 Tablespoon *(13 g)* ghee
- ½ teaspoon *(1 g)* chili powder *(optional)*
- ½ teaspoon *(1 g)* paprika *(optional)*
- 1 teaspoon *(5 ml)* hot sauce
- ½ teaspoon *(1 g)* mustard powder *(optional)*
- Stevia equivalent to ½ Tablespoon *(6 g)* of sugar *(optional)*

INSTRUCTIONS

1. Place all ingredients into a saucepan. Heat on a medium heat for a few minutes while stirring.

Caesar Dressing

Prep Time: 15 minutes
Cook Time: 0 minutes
Total Time: 15 minutes
Yield: approx. 1 cup
Serving Size: approx. 1/8 cup

Back before we were Paleo, we used to eat low-carb, and that often meant a lot of Caesar salads. We didn't know it at the time, but those dressings contain incredible amounts of terrible oils *(like canola, corn, vegetable, etc.)*. This recipe tastes just as good and doesn't have any of those bad oils.

INGREDIENTS

- 2 egg yolks
- 6 anchovies
- 1 cup *(8 fl oz, 240 ml)* coconut oil, melted
- 2 teaspoons *(9 g)* Dijon mustard
- 2 large garlic cloves, crushed
- 4 Tablespoons *(60 ml)* apple cider vinegar
- ¼ teaspoon *(1 g)* salt
- ¼ teaspoon *(1 g)* freshly ground black pepper

INSTRUCTIONS

1. Blend or whisk the 2 egg yolks with the apple cider vinegar.

2. Slowly add in the coconut oil while blending until it forms a mayo texture.

3. Add in rest of the oil, the anchovies, mustard, salt, and pepper and blend well.

Cajun Seasoning

Prep Time: 5 minutes
Cook Time: 0 minutes
Total Time: 5 minutes
Yield: 6 Tablespoons
Serving: N/A *(to be used in other recipes)*

Cajun food is Jeremy's favorite - he loves food that's incredibly flavorful. Some Cajun seasoning you can buy in stores is OK *(be sure to check ingredients carefully)*, but we prefer making our own. You can also control the spiciness this way.

INGREDIENTS

- 1½ Tablespoons *(10 g)* paprika
- 1½ Tablespoons *(13 g)* garlic powder
- ½ Tablespoons *(3 g)* onion powder
- ½ Tablespoons *(3 g)* black pepper
- 1 teaspoon *(2 g)* cayenne pepper
- 1 teaspoon *(2 g)* dried oregano
- 1 teaspoon *(1 g)* dried thyme
- 1 teaspoon *(1 g)* dried basil
- 1-2 teaspoons *(6-12 g)* of salt *(to taste)*

INSTRUCTIONS

1. Mix all the dried spices and herbs together and store in an airtight jar.

Coconut Mayonnaise

Prep Time: 15 minutes
Cook Time: 0 minutes
Total Time: 15 minutes
Yield: 1 cup
Serving Size: N/A *(use in other recipes)*

When we started planning this cookbook, we weren't initially planning on including a mayonnaise recipe, but you'd be surprised just how many other recipes need mayo *(or at least how many are made better by its presence)*. This recipe takes just 15 minutes, and you'll use it all the time.

INGREDIENTS

- 2 egg yolks
- 2 Tablespoons *(30 ml)* of apple cider vinegar
- 1 cup *(240 ml)* coconut oil, melted *(but not too hot)*

INSTRUCTIONS

1. Blend or whisk the 2 egg yolks with the 2 Tablespoons *(30 ml)* of apple cider vinegar.
2. Slowly add in the coconut oil while blending *(I used a blender and added in the coconut oil from the hole at top of the blender approximately 1/2 tablespoon at a time until it forms a mayo texture).*
3. Add in rest of the oil (and a bit more if you want a less thick texture) and blend well.
4. Use immediately *(if you want to store it in the fridge, then use 1/2 cup olive oil and 1/2 cup coconut oil instead of only coconut oil, as the coconut oil will make the mayo solidify in the fridge).*
We try to use it within a week.

SUBSTITUTIONS

- Olive oil can be used instead of coconut oil.
- Spices and herbs can be added for different types of mayo.
- Lemon juice can be used instead of apple cider vinegar (but it gives a different taste to the mayo).

Coconut Ranch Dressing

Prep Time: 10 minutes
Cook Time: 0 minutes
Total Time: 10 minutes
Yield: ½ cup
Serving Size: N/A

Ranch dressing is another condiment that has so many uses. From chicken wings to salads, it's something that we often need to use when we're making a party dish.

INGREDIENTS

- ¼ cup *(60 ml)* of coconut mayo *(see page 172 for recipe)*
- ¼ cup *(60 ml)* coconut milk
- 1 clove of garlic, crushed
- ½ teaspoon *(1 g)* onion powder
- 1 Tablespoon *(4 g)* fresh parsley, finely chopped *(or 1 tsp (0.5 g) dried parsley)*
- 1 Tablespoon *(3 g)* fresh chives, finely chopped *(or omit)*
- 1 teaspoon *(1 g)* fresh dill, finely chopped *(or 1/2 tsp (0.5 g) dried dill)*
- Dash of salt
- Dash of pepper

INSTRUCTIONS

1. Mix together the mayo, coconut milk, onion powder, salt, and pepper with a fork.
2. Gently mix in the garlic and fresh herbs.

Honey Mustard Dressing

Prep Time: 5 minutes
Cook Time: 0 minutes
Total Time: 5 minutes
Yield: 1/3 cup
Serving Size: N/A *(used as condiment for other dishes)*

It always seemed to us like all honey mustard dressing should just be is honey and mustard. After all, isn't that yummy enough? As it turns out, most honey mustard dressings have a ton of other things we don't want in them. So we made our own. *(We also included a couple things that make it taste much better, but they're 100% Paleo.)*

INGREDIENTS
- 4 Tablespoons *(56 g)* Dijon mustard
- 2 Tablespoons *(42 g)* raw honey, slightly melted *(adjust amount to taste)*
- 1 ½ teaspoons *(3 g)* ginger powder
- 1 ½ teaspoons *(7 ml)* apple cider vinegar

INSTRUCTIONS
1. Mix all ingredients together in a bowl.
2. Store in an airtight glass jar or container in refrigerator. *(Typically lasts for 2-4 weeks.)*

Spice-filled Ketchup

Prep Time: 10 minutes
Cook Time: 0 minues
Total Time: 10 minutes
Yield: approx. ¾ cup
Serving Size: N/A (used as condiment for other dishes)

Before we went Paleo, Jeremy used to put ketchup on pretty much everything. He doesn't do it so much any longer, since we now both appreciate the natural tastes of food a lot more. However, for certain foods *(like our Popcorn Shrimp)*, ketchup is still a big difference-maker.

INGREDIENTS

- 1 6-ounce *(170 g)* can of tomato paste
- 1/3 cup *(80 ml)* water *(add more if you want a more "liquid-y" ketchup)*
- 1 Tablespoon *(15 ml)* apple cider vinegar
- ½ Tablespoon *(4 g)* garlic powder
- ½ Tablespoon *(3 g)* onion powder
- 1 teaspoon *(2 g)* gelatin powder *(optional)*
- 1 teaspoon *(3 g)* cinnamon
- ½ teaspoon *(1 g)* nutmeg
- ½ teaspoon *(4 g)* raw honey
- ¼ teaspoon *(0.5 g)* cloves

INSTRUCTIONS

1. Heat a saucepan on the stove on medium heat and add in the water and tomato paste. Stir well.
2. Then add in the rest of the ingredients and stir until fully combined.
3. Cool and store in airtight glass jars in the fridge *(it should last 2-4 weeks)*.

Strawberry Salad Dressing

Prep Time: 10 minutes
Cook Time: 0 minutes
Total Time: 10 minutes
Yield: 4 servings
Serving Size: 1 ounce *(approx.)*

If you're just starting a Paleo diet, you absolutely must have a couple really good salad dressing recipes. Salads are an excellent way to get more veggies into your diet, and as much as meat is paraded in Paleo, veggies are hugely important.

INGREDIENTS

- 3 strawberries
- 1 teaspoon *(7 g)* raw honey
- 1/3 cup *(80 ml)* of olive oil
- 1 Tablespoon *(15 ml)* apple cider vinegar
- ¼ teaspoon *(1 g)* paprika *(omit for AIP)*
- 1 Tablespoon *(8 g)* sesame seeds *(omit for AIP)*

INSTRUCTIONS

1. Place all ingredients into a blender and blend well.

SUBSTITUTIONS

- Other berries can be used instead of strawberries
- Other Paleo sugars can be used instead of raw honey.
- Balsamic vinegar can be used instead of apple cider vinegar.

Chocolate Almond Butter Spread

Prep Time: 10 minutes
Cook Time: 0 minutes
Total Time: 10 minutes
Yield: 1/2 cup

If you love nutella, then give this chocolate almond butter spread instead. Spread some on some Paleo bread for a delicious snack.

INGREDIENTS

- 1/4 cup almond butter
- 2 Tablespoons cacao powder
- 2 Tablespoons coconut sugar
- 1-2 Tablespoons coconut cream or coconut milk
- Dash of salt

INSTRUCTIONS

1. Mix all the ingredients together. Add in sufficient coconut cream or coconut milk to make the mixture spreadable.

SUBSTITUTIONS

- Hazelnut butter can be used instead of almond butter.

Ghee in Slow Cooker

Prep Time: 0 minutes
Cook Time: 3 hours
Total Time: 3 hours
Yield: 10 oz

If you don't have access to ghee, then you can make it yourself in the slow cooker (you can of course also make it on the stove on very low heat). Use better quality (unsalted) butter for a better tasting ghee.

INGREDIENTS
- 16 oz (454 g) butter

INSTRUCTIONS
1. Place butter into slow cooker and place lid on (slightly ajar so that the steam escapes).
2. Turn slow cooker on low for 2-3 hours until milk solids brown and fall to the bottom and bubbles slow down.
3. Place the cheesecloth at the top of the funnel and the funnel end into the mason jar.
4. Pour ghee through the cheesecloth through the funnel into the mason jars and store in fridge.

SUBSTITUTIONS
• You can flavor your ghee with vanilla and spices.

Crunchy Kale Chips

Prep Time: 5 minutes
Cooking Time: varies *(depending on cooking method)*
Total Time: varies *(depending on cooking method)*
Yield: 2 servings
Serving Size: 1 bowl

We first made these chips because we'd bought something similar in a grocery store. But kale chips in grocery stores are always so expensive *(and not always Paleo)*. These are easy, and they taste fantastic.

INGREDIENTS

- 4 large kale leaves
- ½ Tablespoon *(9 g)* salt
- 2 Tablespoons *(30 ml)* olive oil
- ¼ Tablespoon *(1 g)* crushed red pepper *(optional) (omit if AIP)*
- ½ Tablespoon *(4 g)* paprika *(optional) (omit if AIP)*

INSTRUCTIONS

1. Wash the kale leaves and remove the stems so you're just left with the leaves. Dry the leaves well.
2. In a bowl, add the leaves and the salt, olive oil, and spices. Mix well.
3. If using the oven, preheat oven to 300 F *(150 C)* and place the leaves flat on a baking tray *(with no overlapping)*. Bake for 5-10 minutes - make sure the leaves get crispy but not burned.
4. If using a dehydrator, place the leaves flat on the dehydrator trays *(with no overlapping)* and dehydrate until crispy on 135 F *(57 C) (for 3-5 hours)*.
5. If using a microwave, place the leaves on a microwavable plate and place in microwave on full power for 2-3 minutes *(check after 2 minutes to make sure they aren't burning - you may need to test the time and power for your microwave settings)*.

K D A

Easy Guacamole

Prep Time: 10 minutes
Cooking Time: 0 minutes
Total Time: 10 minutes
Yield: 2 servings
Serving Size: 1/2 cup *(approx.)*

We haven't made much guacamole recently, but when we were thinking about recipes to put into this cookbook, we remembered that this used to be one of our favorites. We'd forgotten it just because we cook and prepare so many other things, but I have a feeling we'll be eating more guacamole in the near future.

INGREDIENTS

- 2 ripe avocados
- 1 small tomato, diced
- ¼ cup *(4 g)* cilantro, finely chopped
- Juice from half a lime
- Salt to taste
- 1 jalapeño, finely chopped *(optional)*
- 1 teaspoon *(3 g)* chili powder *(optional)*

INSTRUCTIONS

1. Cut the avocados in half, remove the stone in the middle, and scoop out the flesh into a bowl.
2. Mash up the avocado flesh using a spoon or fork.
3. Add in the tomatoes, cilantro, lime juice, salt to taste, jalapeño, and chili powder.
4. Mix well.

Macadamia Almond Granola Bar

Prep Time: 15 minutes
Cook Time: 2 hours refrigeration
Total Time: 2 hours 15 minutes
Yield: 10 servings
Serving Size: 1 bar

Every time we go into a grocery store, we see dozens of different snack bars, and 99% of them contain ingredients we'd never eat. That's why we first made our own a few years ago. You can substitute a lot of different nuts, seeds, and dried fruits to make a variety of different flavors.

INGREDIENTS

- ¼ cup *(30 g)* almonds
- ¼ cup *(30 g)* macadamia nuts
- ¼ cup *(30 g)* pumpkin seeds
- ¼ cup *(30 g)* pecans
- 20 pitted dates, processed in a food processor to form a paste
- 3 Tablespoons *(45 ml)* coconut oil, melted
- Dash of salt

INSTRUCTIONS

1. *(Microwave the dates for 30 seconds if they are cold and hard.)* Pulse the almonds, macadamia nuts, pumpkin seeds, pecans, dates, and salt together in a food processor or blender (if using a thermomix, blend on setting 5 for a few seconds).
2. The nuts and seeds should be chopped and the dates should form a paste. When you squeeze the mixture together, it should start to stick together.
3. Mix in the coconut oil.
4. Form into a long flat bar using your hands and some parchment paper. *If you have trouble getting the mixture to stick together, try adding more dates or raw honey or maple syrup (but this will make it sweeter).*
5. Refrigerate for 2 hours before cutting into smaller bars *(approx. 10 bars)*.

SUBSTITUTIONS

- Other nuts and seeds can be used instead.

Salted Pretzel Bites

Prep Time: 15 minutes
Cook Time: 15 minutes
Total Time: 30 minutes
Yield: 4 servings
Serving Size: 7 pretzel bites *(approx.)*

If you or your family are looking for an easy snack or treat, these pretzel bites will turn out well every time, as they're almost impossible to mess up *(unless you burn them)*.

INGREDIENTS

- 3 eggs
- 1½ cups *(143 g)* almond flour
- 2 Tablespoons *(30 ml)* ghee, melted
- 3 Tablespoons *(21 g)* coconut flour
- ½ teaspoon *(3 g)* salt
- 1 egg, whisked *(as egg wash)*
- Coarse sea salt for sprinkling *(optional)*

INSTRUCTIONS

1. Preheat oven to 350 F *(177 C)*.
2. Place 3 eggs, almond flour, ghee, coconut flour, and ½ teaspoon salt into a bowl and mix well until it forms a dough.
3. Let the dough sit for 5 minutes.
4. Roll into pretzel bites *(small balls)* and place on a parchment paper lined baking tray.
5. Bake in oven for 6-7 minutes.
6. Take the pretzels out and heat oven to 400 F *(204 C)*.
7. Turn each pretzel bite over, brush some of the whisked egg onto the top, and sprinkle some of the coarse sea salt on them.
8. Bake for 5 more minutes.

Savory Italian Crackers

Prep Time: 15 minutes
Cook Time: 10 minutes
Total Time: 25 minutes
Yield: 4 servings
Serving Size: 5 crackers *(approx.)*

One of the things people often miss most when starting a Paleo diet is the "crunch" of various foods. These crackers are an easy way to get that experience back in a Paleo way. This also goes great with the Oregano Raspberry Liver Pate *(see page 184 for recipe)*.

INGREDIENTS

- 1½ cups *(143 g)* almond flour
- 1 egg
- 2 Tablespoons *(30 ml)* olive oil
- ¾ teaspoon *(5 g)* salt
- ¼ teaspoon *(0.5 g)* basil
- ½ teaspoon *(1 g)* thyme
- ¼ teaspoon *(0.5 g)* oregano
- ½ teaspoon *(1 g)* onion powder
- ¼ teaspoon *(0.5 g)* garlic powder

INSTRUCTIONS

1. Preheat oven to 350 F *(177 C)*.
2. Mix all the ingredients well to form a dough.
3. Shape dough into a long rectangular log (use some foil or cling film to pack the dough tight) and then cut into thin slices *(approximately 0.2 inches (0.5 cm) thick)*. Gently place each slice onto a parchment paper lined baking tray. It makes approx. 20-30 crackers, depending on size.
4. Bake for 10-12 minutes.

SUBSTITUTIONS

• Italian seasoning can be used instead of basil, thyme, oregano, onion powder, and garlic powder if you don't have those available.
• Other nut flours can be used instead of almond flour (just food process the nuts using a food processor or blender into a fine meal).

Oregano Raspberry Liver Pate

Prep Time: 10 minutes
Cooking Time: 20 minutes
Total Time: 30 minutes
Yield: 4 servings
Serving Size: 2-3 Tablespoons *(approx.)*

Chicken liver is easy to find and very nutritious. Try this pate with the Savory Italian Crackers *(see page 183 for recipe)*.

INGREDIENTS

- 0.7 lb (317g) chicken liver
- 2 Tablespoons *(30 ml)* ghee *(may need extra)*
- ½ onion, chopped
- Approx. 50 oregano leaves
- 15 raspberries (optional) - makes the pate less smooth
- Salt to taste

INSTRUCTIONS

1. Melt 2 tablespoons of ghee in a pan and saute the chopped onions and chicken liver until the liver is cooked (just pink inside). This takes 10-15 minutes on medium heat, and you may find putting a lid onto the pan for 5 minutes at the end helps.

2. Add in the oregano leaves a few minutes before the liver is done.

3. Blend the liver, onions, oregano, raspberries, and salt until smooth (add in an extra tablespoon of ghee if needed to make the pate smoother).

SUBSTITUTIONS

- Other herbs and spices can be used instead of the oregano and raspberries.

Tropical Mango Salsa

Prep Time: 15 minutes
Cooking Time: 0 minutes
Total Time: 15 minutes
Yield: 4 servings
Serving Size: ½ cup (approx.)

We don't make this very often, but we're not sure why. This salsa is spectacular, and it actually goes with a lot of different meats and dishes *(pork in particular)*.

INGREDIENTS

- 2 Ataulfo mangoes, diced
- 2 small tomatoes, diced
- 1 bell pepper, diced
- ¼ cup *(4 g)* cilantro, finely chopped
- 4 cloves of garlic, minced
- 2 jalapeño peppers, diced (optional but strongly encouraged)
- 2 Tablespoons *(30 ml)* lime juice
- 1 Tablespoon *(15 ml)* lemon juice
- 1 teaspoon *(6 g)* salt

INSTRUCTIONS

1. Mix all the ingredients together well.
2. Serve chilled.

SUBSTITUTIONS

- Peach, nectarines, or apples, can be used instead of *(or in addition to)* mangos for a different flavor.

Chapter 7: Beverages

Coconut Masala Chai

Prep Time: 5 minutes
Cook Time: 5 minutes
Total Time: 10 minutes
Yield: 2 servings
Serving Size: 1 cup

We visited India in early 2014. It was an amazing place, and the history of food and cooking there is astonishing. But too many recipes now use a ton of sugar, pasteurized milk, and seed oils. Masala Chai Tea is something that was served everywhere we went *(and Louise LOVES tea)*, so when we got back, we knew that we needed to make our own version.

INGREDIENTS
- 1 cup *(240 ml)* coconut cream *(or, alternatively use the top layer of cream from a refrigerated can of coconut milk)*
- 1 cup *(240 ml)* water
- 1 teaspoon *(7 g)* raw honey *(or other sweetener of choice or can be increased or omitted)*
- 1 Tablespoon *(2 g)* loose black tea leaves
- Pinch of masala tea spice blend *(recipe below or purchase on Amazon here)*

Masala Tea Spice Blend
- 1 Tablespoon *(7 g)* nutmeg
- 1 Tablespoon *(5 g)* ginger powder
- 1 Tablespoon *(6 g)* cardamom
- 1 Tablespoon *(6 g)* black pepper
- 1 Tablespoon *(8 g)* cinnamon
- 1 teaspoon *(2 g)* cloves
- 1 Tablespoon *(5 g)* dried basil *(optional)*, ground into a powder

INSTRUCTIONS
1. Heat the coconut cream and water in a saucepan.
2. Add in the honey/sweetener, the tea, and the spice blend. Mix well.
3. Heat at a low simmer for approx. 4-5 minutes.
4. Taste the tea and add more honey/sweetener or spices to taste.
5. Pour through a strainer *(to remove the tea leaves)* and serve immediately.

Ginger Basil Tea

Prep Time: 5 minutes
Cook Time: 0 minutes
Total Time: 5 minutes
Yield: 1 serving
Serving Size: 1 cup of tea

You should know that Louise really couldn't imagine living without tea. She's truly British at heart (she did grow up in England, after all). Ginger is very commonly added to tea, but the basil really makes all the difference here. Jeremy even likes this one…

INGREDIENTS

- 2 cups *(480 ml)* boiling water
- ½ teaspoon *(1 g)* fresh ginger, grated *(or 10 very thin slices of ginger)*
- 4 fresh basil leaves

INSTRUCTIONS

1. Add the ginger and basil to a cup or teapot and pour boiling water into the cup/teapot.
2. Brew for 5 minutes.
3. Press the basil leaves gently with a spoon to get more flavor out of them, if desired.
4. Sieve out *(using a special teapot or a strainer)* the ginger and basil.
5. Enjoy hot or cold.

Pumpkin Spice Latte

Prep Time: 5 minutes
Cook Time: 0 minutes
Total Time: 5 minutes
Yield: 1 serving
Serving Size: 1 cup of coffee

Normally, our drinks are limited to water *(and, for Louise, coffee and tea)*. But during the winter *(and especially around the holidays)*, Louise likes to "spice it up" a little, and this Pumpkin Spice Latte is the result.

INGREDIENTS

- 1 cup *(240 ml)* black coffee
- 1 Tablespoon *(15 g)* pumpkin puree
- ¼ teaspoon *(1 g)* cinnamon
- ¼ teaspoon *(1 g)* nutmeg
- Dash of cloves
- 1 Tablespoon *(15 ml)* ghee

INSTRUCTIONS

- Place all the ingredients into a blender and blend well for 15 seconds.

The Ultimate Frothy Coffee

Prep Time: 5 minutes
Cook Time: 0 minutes
Total Time: 5 minutes
Yield: 1 serving
Serving Size: 1 mug

If you're used to drinking coffee with milk and sugar, then this is a recipe that will change your life. It may not sound great at first, but once you try it, it's more filling, gives you the same coffee kick, and also tastes even better. Louise now drinks this almost every day.

INGREDIENTS

- ½ Tablespoon *(7 g)* ghee
- ½ Tablespoon *(7 g)* coconut oil
- 1-2 cups *(240-480 ml)* of whatever coffee you like *(or black or rooibos tea)*
- 1 Tablespoon *(15 ml)* almond milk or coconut milk

INSTRUCTIONS

1. Put the ghee, coconut oil, almond milk *(or coconut milk)*, and the coffee into a blender *(use less ghee and coconut oil if you are not used to a lot of fat in your diet)*.
2. Blend for 5-10 seconds. The coffee turns into a foamy, creamy color. Pour it into your favorite coffee cup and enjoy!
3. If you don't have a blender, then try using a milk frother *(you can often find them for under $5 in various stores)*.

Coconut Milk Hot Chocolate

Prep Time: 5 minutes
Cook Time: 0 minutes
Total Time: 5 minutes
Yield: 1 serving
Serving Size: 1 mug

This is the basic recipe for a coconut milk hot chocolate drink. You can spice it up with some cinnamon or add in peppermint extract to make peppermint hot chocolate.

INGREDIENTS

- 1/3 cup *(1 oz or 30 g)* unsweetened cacao powder
- 2 Tablespoons *(24 g)* coconut sugar
- 1/3 cup *(80 ml)* boiling water
- 3 Tablespoons *(45 ml)* coconut cream (from top of refrigerated can of coconut milk)

INSTRUCTIONS

1. Place the cacao powder and coconut sugar into a mug and add in the boiling water. Mix until it's all dissolved.
2. Add in the coconut cream and stir well.

Lemon Thyme Infused Iced Tea

Prep Time: 10 minutes + overnight infusion
Cook Time: 0 minutes
Total Time: 10 minutes
Yield: 6-8 serving
Serving Size: 1 cup

We grow lemon thyme in the garden, and this lemon thyme iced tea is so refreshing in the summer.

INGREDIENTS
- 4-6 cups of black tea
- 6 sprigs of lemon thyme

INSTRUCTIONS
1. Brew the black tea until ready.
2. Remove the tea bag(s) and add 2 sprigs of lemon thyme into the hot tea.
3. Let cool and then refrigerate overnight.
4. Remove the lemon thyme and serve with ice and fresh sprigs of lemon thyme for decoration.

SUBSTITUTIONS
- Juice from 1/2 lemon and sprigs of thyme can be used instead of lemon thyme.

Coconut Iced Tea Latte

Prep Time: 10 minutes
Cook Time: 0 minutes
Total Time: 10 minutes
Yield: 2 servings
Serving Size: 1 cup

This is the Paleo version of the classic iced tea latte.

INGREDIENTS

- 2 cups *(500 ml)* black tea
- 3 Tablespoons *(30 ml)* coconut milk (or to taste)
- 2 Tablespoons *(24 g)* coconut sugar (or to taste) (omit for D)

INSTRUCTIONS

1. Brew the black tea until ready.
2. Add in the coconut milk and coconut sugar to taste.
3. Blend for a few seconds or use a milk frother.
4. Pour into a glass with ice.

SUBSTITUTIONS

• Almond milk can be used instead of coconut milk.

Sinh To Bo (Vietnamese Smoothie)

Prep Time: 5 minutes
Cook Time: 0 minutes
Total Time: 5 minutes
Yield: 1 serving
Serving Size: 1 glass

This is the Paleo version of the classic iced tea latte.

INGREDIENTS

- 1 avocado
- 1 cup *(500 g)* ice
- ½ cup *(250 ml)* coconut milk - add a little bit more if you have trouble getting the mixture to blend
- 1 Tablespoon *(21 g)* raw honey - add more to taste

INSTRUCTIONS

1. Cut a ripe avocado in half.
2. Use a spoon to scoop out the avocado flesh.
3. Place the avocado flesh into the blender with the ice, coconut milk, and honey, and blend well (start slow and increase the speed slowly).
4. Add more coconut milk if necessary to blend until smooth.

SUBSTITUTIONS

• Almond milk can be used instead of coconut milk.

Recommended Websites

OUR 9 FAVORITE SITES

http://PaleoMagazine.com *[Our own website]*
Recipes + Health & Nutrition

http://ThePaleoMom.com
Recipes + Health & Nutrition

http://ChrisKresser.com
Health & Nutrition

http://MarksDailyApple.com
Health & Nutrition

http://PaleOMG.com
Recipes

http://CivilizedCavemanCooking.com
Recipes

http://PaleoParents.com
Recipes

http://CookEatPaleo.com
Recipes

http://PaleoForWomen.com
Health & Nutrition

ADDITIONAL AWESOME SITES

http://Ancestralize.me
Health & Nutrition

http://RubiesandRadishes.com
Recipes

http://BrittanyAngell.com
Recipes

http://CaveGirlEats.com
Recipes + Health & Nutrition

http://ElanasPantry.com
Recipes

http://AGirlWorthSaving.com
Recipes

http://HollywoodHomestead.com
Recipes

http://PaleoCupboard.com
Recipes

http://BeautyandtheFoodie.com
Recipes

http://PaleoParents.com
Recipes + Health & Nutrition

http://PracticalPaleo.Blogspot.com
Recipes

http://PrimalPalate.com
Recipes

http://MyHeartBeets.com
Recipes

http://RobbWolf.com
Health & Nutrition

http://PaleoFoodieKitchen.com
Recipes

http://TheCuriousCoconut.com
Recipes

http://TheClothesMaketheGirl.com
Recipes + Health & Nutrition

http://TheDomesticMan.com
Recipes

http://ThePaleoMama.com
Health & Nutrition

http://TheSpunkyCoconut.com
Recipes

http://StupidEasyPaleo.com
Recipes

http://PredominantlyPaleo.com
Recipes

http://ZenBelly.com
Recipes

Recipe Index

CPSIA information can be obtained
at www.ICGtesting.com
Printed in the USA
FSOW04n0148130916
24879FS